ach®
yourself

AutoCAD 2007

teach® yourself

AutoCAD 2007
mac bride

For UK order enquiries: please contact Bookpoint Ltd, 130 Milton Park, Abingdon, Oxon OX14 4SB. Telephone: +44 (0) 1235 827720. Fax: +44 (0) 1235 400454. Lines are open 09.00–17.00, Monday to Saturday, with a 24-hour message answering service. Details about our titles and how to order are available at www.teachyourself.co.uk

For USA order enquiries: please contact McGraw-Hill Customer Services, PO Box 545, Blacklick, OH 43004-0545, USA. Telephone: 1-800-722-4726. Fax: 1-614-755-5645.

For Canada order enquiries: please contact McGraw-Hill Ryerson Ltd, 300 Water St, Whitby, Ontario L1N 9B6, Canada. Telephone: 905 430 5000. Fax: 905 430 5020.

Long renowned as the authoritative source for self-guided learning – with more than 50 million copies sold worldwide – the **teach yourself** series includes over 500 titles in the fields of languages, crafts, hobbies, business, computing and education.

British Library Cataloguing in Publication Data: a catalogue record for this title is available from the British Library.

Library of Congress Catalog Card Number: on file.

First published in UK 2006 by Hodder Education, 338 Euston Road, London NW1 3BH.

First published in US 2006 by The McGraw-Hill Companies, Inc.

This edition published 2006.

The **teach yourself** name is a registered trade mark of Hodder Headline.

Computer hardware and software brand names mentioned in this book are protected by their respective trademarks and are acknowledged.

Typeset by MacDesign, Southampton

Printed in Great Britain for Hodder Education, a division of Hodder Headline, 338 Euston Road, London NW1 3BH, by Cox & Wyman Ltd, Reading, Berkshire.

The publisher has used its best endeavours to ensure that the URLs for external websites referred to in this book are correct and active at the time of going to press. However, the publisher and the author have no responsibility for the websites and can make no guarantee that a site will remain live or that the content will remain relevant, decent or appropriate.

Hodder Headline's policy is to use papers that are natural, renewable and recyclable products and made from wood grown in sustainable forests. The logging and manufacturing processes are expected to conform to the environmental regulations of the country of origin.

Impression number   10 9 8 7 6 5 4 3 2 1

Year   2010 2009 2008 2007 2006

v

contents

preface

AutoCAD is the world's leading Computer Aided Design (CAD) software, used by architects, engineers, designers and other professionals to create 2D or 3D drawings and models. It is a very powerful and sophisticated package, capable of handling the most complex constructions, but it is also well-designed and logical, and so not too hard to get started with.

The aim of this book is to introduce AutoCAD's key tools and techniques. It assumes that you have enough understanding of Windows to be able to start a program, save and open files, and use the Internet. A high level of Windows competence is not needed – and in fact, may not help. AutoCAD started life in the days before Windows, and some of its operations will not seem intuitive to people who have only ever used Windows software.

AutoCAD is a huge package, and this is a small book, so I have had to be very selective about what has gone in. I hope that you will find here the grounding that you need to get started and the confidence to go on and explore more of the potential of the system.

Mac Bride
2006

01

introducing AutoCAD

In this chapter you will learn:

- about the AutoCAD tools
- how to use the Command Line window
- how to specify coordinates
- about handling files in AutoCAD

Starting AutoCAD

AutoCAD can be started from its Start menu entry –
you should find it in the Autodesk submenu – or from
its Desktop shortcut.

AutoCAD 2007

When the AutoCAD window first opens, it should display a blank
drawing ready for you to start work on a new project.

The AutoCAD window

The main areas and features of the AutoCAD window are marked
on the screenshot on page 3. Note these, in particular:

- The **Drawing area** can display model or paper layout space.
  Click on the tags at the bottom left to switch displays.

- The **Command Line window** is used for entering coordinates.
  Commands can also be entered here, though it is often simpler to use the menus or toolbars.

- The **Status bar** shows the coordinates of the cursor at the
  bottom left. In the centre and the right of the bar are toggles
  (on/off switches) for some key options. Note these two:

  If **Grid** is on, a rectangular pattern of dots is shown. These
  are normally 10 units apart.

  If **Snap** is on, the mouse jumps to the nearest snap point when
  you click.

The toolbars

AutoCAD has over 30 toolbars. These six are probably the most
used.

- The **Standard** toolbar contains the same filing, printing and
  copying tools that you will find in most Windows applications, plus tools to move and zoom around a drawing, and
  ones to turn the more-used palettes on and off.

- The **Properties** toolbar is used for setting the colour, weight
  and style of lines (see Chapter 4).

- The **Draw** toolbar holds the most commonly used drawing
  tools. The full set can be found in the Draw menu. We will

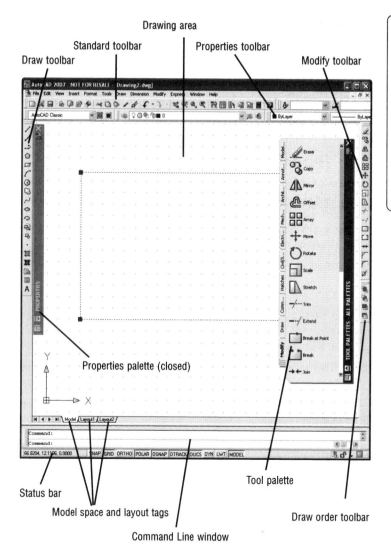

Drawing area

Standard toolbar

Properties toolbar

Draw toolbar

Modify toolbar

Properties palette (closed)

Tool palette

Status bar

Model space and layout tags

Draw order toolbar

Command Line window

Figure 1.1 The AutoCAD window when it first opens. Notice the tabs at the bottom of the working area. Drawings are created in model space (on the Model tab). The Layout tabs are used for plotting – leave these well alone until you are ready to start thinking about outputting your work to paper. We will come to them in Chapter 10.

look at the Line tool later in this chapter, then return to the rest in Chapter 2.

◆ The four tools on the **Draw order** toolbar let you adjust the order of overlapping objects.

◆ The **Modify** toolbar has tools for moving, rotating, mirroring and otherwise manipulating objects.

◆ The **Dimensions** toolbar has tools for marking dimensions on your drawings (see Chapter 7).

The toolbar layout is not fixed and can be easily changed to suit your current drawing. Toolbars can be turned on or off, and can be moved to new positions. A toolbar can be docked at the top or either side of the drawing area, or allowed to float anywhere on screen. Floating toolbars can have their tools in one long single line, or in a short multi-line block.

To turn toolbars on or off: .

1 Right-click on any toolbar and the full list will appear. Those toolbars currently displayed will have ticks by their names.

2 Click on a toolbar name to toggle its display on or off.

To move a toolbar:

1 If the toolbar is docked against an edge, click on the double raised lines at the left/top. If it is floating, click on its title bar.

2 Drag the toolbar across the screen. An outline will appear to show its shape if placed at that point. If the toolbar is going to float, the outline will be drawn in a heavier line and will be a larger shape – as there will be a title bar.

3 Release the mouse button when you are in the right place. If the toolbar is being docked, it will automatically go to the left or the top of the docking area.

4 Toolbars can be moved within a docking area if required. Drag on the raised lines and release the outline when it is over the place where you want it to go.

To resize a floating toolbar:

1 Move the cursor over the side or bottom of the toolbar until it turns into a double-headed arrow.

2 Drag the arrow to change the shape of the toolbar.

Figure 1.2 Toolbars can be moved and resized easily.

The palettes

A palette is a kind of cross between a toolbar and a dialog box. AutoCAD's 14 palettes provide alternative routes to commands, options and information. They are particularly useful where you need to maximize the visible working area as one palette can replace a dozen or more toolbars.

The most valuable palettes – and the first three on the Tools menu – are:

- The **Dashboard** holds all the essential tools for modelling and rendering in 3D (see Chapter 12).

- The **Properties** palette displays and allows you to change the properties of the currently selected object(s).

- The **Tool Palettes** hold different sets of tools, giving you access to all the essential tools for a variety of jobs. This is a set of palettes fitted into one structure, and has extra commands on the shortcut menu to control its contents. The palettes are accessed by clicking on their name tabs – if the name is not visible, click on the edge of the tab for a list of available palettes.

To display a palette:

1 Open the **Tools** menu, point to **Palettes** and click on the one you want.

Or

2 Use the **[Ctrl] + [number key]** combination to open it.

The most used ones have [Ctrl] + key combinations

By default, the palettes float over the working area, but can be anchored to the left or right up against the frame. When floating or anchored, if a palette is in Auto-hide mode, it will shrink back to a title bar when the cursor moves off it, opening up again when the cursor is held over.

Typical palette   Close

Identifying icon

The shortcut menu on most palettes
controls the display and position only

Locks the palette to the window frame

Auto-hide shrinks a palette down to its
title bar when the mouse is not on it

If on, shows a description of selected
option at the bottom of the palette

Tool palettes

Click to bring
the palette to
the front

Move slider to reach tools off
the top/bottom of the display

Change the
tool set

Current palette

Display all palettes

The mouse in AutoCAD

AutoCAD makes more use of the mouse than most Windows applications do. The left button works as normal, but note the double-click:

* Click to select a tool or a drawn object, as usual.

* Click and drag to draw a line or shape, or to enclose and select a set of objects.

* Double-click on a drawn object to open its Properties panel.

A right button click on any object opens its context menu, as normal, but the button can be configured so that a quick click has the same effect as an **[Enter]** keypress. As [Enter] is used so much in AutoCAD, this option should be turned on. Here's how.

To customize the right button:

1 Open the **Tools** menu and select **Options...**

2 Go to the **User Preferences** tab.

Figure 1.3   The User Preferences tab of the Options dialog box. Any of the settings can be changed at any time, but most are best left at their defaults at first. You might like to go to the Display tab where you can set the screen colour and other aspects of the display – I prefer a white background to the default black.

3 In the top right section, click **Right-Click Customization...**

Figure 1.4   Customizing the right-click action.

4 Tick the **Turn on time-sensitive right-click** checkbox.

5 The duration is set for 250 milliseconds. If you find you need a shorter or longer delay, come back to here and change it.

6 Click **Apply & Close.**

7 Back at the **Options** dialog box, click **OK** to close it.

The wheel mouse

If your mouse has a wheel between the buttons, this can be used to zoom and pan around your workspace.

◆ Roll the wheel forward to zoom in.

◆ Roll the wheel backwards to zoom out.

◆ Press the wheel in and drag the mouse to *pan* – to move the drawing within the workspace window.

Model space and paper space

In AutoCAD, drawings are created in *model space*. This can be of any size, measured in any units – metric or imperial, decimal or fractions. You could create a model space to fit inside a matchbox, or to map the west coast rail line from London to Glasgow – and they would both feel much the same within AutoCAD. As the real world dimensions are scaled up or down as necessary to fit into model space, size is almost irrelevant – until you take the plans back to the real world!

You can move around in model space, viewing your drawing from any angle or distance. You can zoom in on details or pull back to see it all at once; you can look at it from a number of pre-set viewpoints or rotate the drawing in any of the three dimensions. Though model space is three-dimensional, the output can only be seen – on screen or on paper – in two dimensions. In practice, most AutoCAD drawings are two-dimensional, because this is what is needed. Drawings can be created in 3D, as you will see, but that takes a little more work than drawing in 2D.

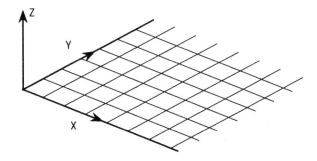

Figure 1.5 Model space is infinite, but you can define the width (X) and length (Y) of the drawing area. The height (Z) is not defined.

Outputs from AutoCAD are in *paper space*. Its size is set by the physical size of the sheets in your plotter or printer. The current screen image can be output to paper, or you can create *layouts*, which show part or all of the drawing, from a given viewpoint. Once a layout is defined, it is more or less fixed (adjustments are possible), but you can define as many as you need.

Starting a drawing

There are three ways to start a new drawing, though two of them may not be available – it all depends upon the Startup setting in the Options. Set it now.

1 Open the **Tools** menu and select **Options...**

2 Go to the **System** tab.

3 In the **General Options** area, at the top right, drop down the **Startup** list and select *Show Startup dialog box*.

4 Click **OK**.

Figure 1.6 Turn on the Startup dialog box for better control over new drawings.

Setting units and limits

Before you can actually start work, you need to specify the units of measurement and the limits of the drawing area.

The drawing units can be:

Decimal   Millimetres

Engineering Feet and inches (with decimals)

Architectural Feet and inches (with fractions)

Fractional Standard units and fractions

Scientific Units, in exponential form

The default drawing limits are 420 by 297. These are suitable for use with A3 paper (420 × 297 mm), giving a simple translation of one drawing unit to one millimetre on paper. If you are using Imperial measurements, the default limits are 12 by 9. The limits can be anything, but if they are very different from the defaults, you may need to change the settings for the grid (page 16), the text (page 93) and the dimension text (page 115).

If the Startup dialog box is turned on, drawings can be started from templates or wizards, or from scratch. (If it is off, you can only start from a template.) There are templates for a range of paper sizes, and for a range of grids and information boxes – explore them at some point. The wizard is a slower way to set values that would otherwise be set through dialog boxes.

We will start from scratch.

1 Click the **New** button ▢ or select **New** from the **File** menu.

2 At the **Create New Drawing** dialog box, click the **Start from scratch** button.

Figure 1.7 Starting from scratch. Explore the templates at some point to see what is available, and note those that have layouts that you are likely to use.

3 Select your **Default Settings – Imperial** or **Metric**.

4 Click **OK**.

5 Open the **Format** menu and select **Units...**

6 At the **Drawing Units** dialog box, the **Length** and **Angle** units are normally *Decimal*. Change these if required.

Figure 1.8 Setting the Drawing Units.

7 **Precision** determines how accurately values are *displayed* (they are *stored* as accurately as possible). Set a level and click **OK**.

8 Open the **Format** menu and select **Drawing Limits**.

9 This does not open a dialog box, but uses the Command Line window to collect the values. You will be prompted for the coordinates of the lower left corner of the drawing area. The current values will be shown in angle brackets, e.g. <0.00,0.00>. Press [Enter] to accept these.

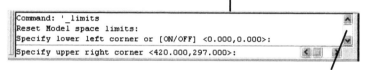

Drag the top bar to change the height of the window

```
Command: '_limits
Reset Model space limits:
Specify lower left corner or [ON/OFF] <0.000,0.000>:
Specify upper right corner <420.000,297.000>:
```

Scroll to view past commands

10 Enter the coordinates of the upper right corner. Give these in the form *width,length*.

Zoom

You can use a wheel mouse to zoom (page 9), but there are also these two tools: **Zoom Window** will expand a selected area to fill the screen; **Zoom Realtime** lets you move in and out flexibly.

To zoom in on a defined window:

1 Click on the **Zoom Window** button 🔍.

2 Drag an outline over the area to be zoomed.

3 Click to fix the far corner.

To zoom in and out:

1 Click on the **Zoom Realtime** button 🔍.

2 Drag the magnifying glass cursor up the screen to zoom in, or down to zoom out.

3 Press [**Escape**] to end zoom mode.

Zoom Realtime   Zoom Window

Figure 1.9 Using the Zoom window.

Drawing with the mouse

Objects are defined by specifying the positions of vertices or by a combination of positions, lengths and angles. They can be drawn with a mouse (or other pointing device) or the data can be typed into the Command Line, or you can use a mixture of both.

When you are drawing, clicking on the working area selects the current position – this is known as *picking*. Freehand drawing can be used for sketching, but it is virtually impossible to position the cursor accurately with any pointing device – look at the coordinates in the Status Bar and you will see that you can never get exactly on any point.

There are two ways to make your mouse work accurate:

- **Snap** – when enabled, the mouse will jump to the nearest snap point when you click. Initially the snap points are the same as the visible grid points. Snap to grid is only useful, of course, if the object's vertices will fit on the grid.

Figure 1.10 Snap makes mouse drawing more accurate.

• **Object Snap** – when enabled, the cursor will jump to the mid or endpoints of an existing line when you click near it.

There is also a **Polar tracking** mode. This shows the distance and angle of the cursor from the last point, but it does not force the cursor to lock onto a specific point as the Snap modes do.

Snap

We saw earlier that the grid, and the Snap mode can be toggled on and off by the Status Bar indicators. You do not need the grid on to use the Snap mode, and the snap and grid points do not have to coincide – though it helps if you snap to a visible grid.

The size of the visible grid and the spacing of the snap points can be adjusted through the Snap and Grid Settings.

1 Open the **Tools** menu and select **Drafting Settings...**

2 Go to the **Snap and Grid** tab.

3 Enter **Snap** and **Grid spacing** values to suit your drawing.

4 Click **OK**.

Figure 1.11 The Snap and Grid spacing values do not need to be the same, and the X and Y values can differ.

Object Snap

When Object Snap is active, you can click accurately onto the end, midpoint, centre or other significant point on an existing object. When the cursor is close to a snap point, a marker appears and the cursor will lock onto it when you click. There are a dozen types of snap points, which can be turned on independently. There is also an option to display the vector (distance and angle) of the cursor from the last drawing point.

The main options are controlled through the Drafting Settings.

1 Open the **Tools** menu and select **Drafting Settings...**

2 At the **Drafting Settings** dialog box, open the **Object Snap** tab.

3 Tick the **Object Snap On** checkbox to activate it.

4 Tick or clear the boxes to select the snap modes to activate.

5 Tick the **Object Snap Tracking On** checkbox if you want the distance and angle vector information.

6 Click **OK**.

Figure 1.12 Activating Object Snap. If you are not going to use a snap mode, turn it off to reduce possible confusion.

Figure 1.13 Using Object Snap. The green (on screen) cross indicates a snap point at the intersection of the rectangle and the arc. The distance and angle data is displayed as tracking is turned on.

Single-use snap

If too many snap modes are active, a multiplicity of markers close together can make life difficult on a complex drawing. In other situations you may normally prefer to work with all snap modes turned off. In either case, there is a single-use snap mode that you can use from the Object Snap toolbar. This will turn on one snap mode while one point is defined.

To use single-use Object Snap:

1 If the Object Snap toolbar is not visible, right-click on any toolbar and tick **Object Snap** in the list of toolbars.

2 Select your drawing tool.

The Object Snap toolbar

Snap to endpoint

Snap to midpoint   Snap to intersection

Snap to centre

3   When it is time to specify a coordinate, click on a snap mode button on the Object Snap toolbar.

4   Using the snap markers as guides, snap to and pick the point.

5   Repeat steps **3** and **4** for picking further points with the same drawing tool.

Specifying coordinates

There are three ways of giving coordinates in the Command Line.

◆   As simple **Cartesian** coordinates, in the form x, y. For example 200,150 specifies a point where x = 200 (i.e. 200 units to the right of 0,0), and y = 150 (i.e. 150 units up from 0,0).

◆   As **relative** coordinates, expressed as the distances from the last point, in the form '@x,y', e.g. @100,-25 specifies a point 100 units to the right and 25 units below the last point.

◆   As **polar** coordinates, giving the distance and angle from the last point, in the form '@distance<angle', e.g. @200<135 means 200 units and 135 degrees from the last point. Angles are normally measured anticlockwise, starting at 3 o'clock.

Figure 1.14   The default angle measurement in AutoCAD. If you prefer to work clockwise, turn on the Clockwise option in the Drawing Units dialog box (page 13).

Feet and inches

If you are working with feet and inches and simply enter a number, AutoCAD will assume it is in inches. To enter a value in feet, type an apostrophe (') after the number.

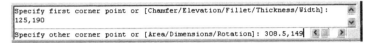

```
Specify first corner point or [Chamfer/Elevation/Fillet/Thickness/Width]:
125,190
Specify other corner point or [Area/Dimensions/Rotation]: 308.5,149
```

Figure 1.15 The Command Window after defining a rectangle. Notice that when the command first started, the system asked for either the first corner point or for an option to be specified. Many AutoCAD commands offer a range of options.

```
Specify first corner point or [Chamfer/Elevation/Fillet/Thickness/Width]:
125,190
Specify other corner point or [Area/Dimensions/Rotation]: @183.5,-51
```

Figure 1.16 These command lines define the same rectangle as the one above, but here the second corner is given in terms of distance from the first.

Tip!

When AutoCAD asks for input through the Command Line, it will sometimes offer default values or options. These will be shown in <angle brackets>. Press [Enter] or right-click to accept the defaults.

The Line tool

Most drawing tools can only be used to draw a single object, and must be reselected to draw another. The Line tool is a little different. It can be used to draw a single line or a continuous sequence, with the endpoint of one being the startpoint of the next.

1 Click the Line tool ✏ on the Draw toolbar.

2 Pick the coordinates by clicking on the drawing area where you want the line to start, or type the coordinates into the Command Line window.

3 Drag across the screen and pick at the end of the line, or type the coordinates.

4 Drag and pick to draw another line, going on from the end-point, or type the next pair of coordinates. Repeat as needed.

5 Press [**Enter**] (or right-click) to stop drawing lines.

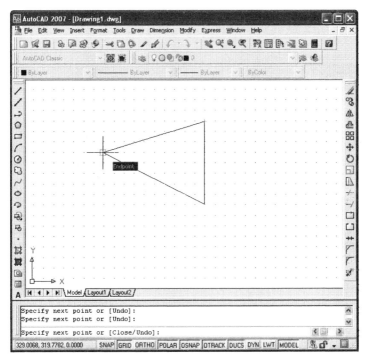

Figure 1.17 Drawing with the Line tool. The pale square at the cross-hairs shows us that Object Snap is on and that the drawing point is over the end of an existing line – the Endpoint label also tells you this.

Selecting and editing lines

Lines can be edited or deleted as needed at any time. First select them. Notice that each line is a separate object, even where they have been drawn in a continuous sequence to produce a shape.

To select a single line:

◆ Click on it.

To select several lines close to each other:

◆ Drag an outline to enclose all or part of the lines – the outline only has to touch a line to select it.

To select scattered lines:

◆ Hold [Shift] and click on each of the lines in turn.

A selected line is shown dashed with blue handles at each end and one at the mid-point.

To move a line:

◆ Click anywhere on the line and drag into the new position.

To stretch or change the angle:

◆ Place the pointer over an end grip (the square handle) and drag to change the angle or length.

To delete a line:

◆ Select it, then press [Delete] or click the **Eraser** tool 🖊.

Dynamic Input

Dynamic Input mode combines the speed and simplicity of mouse work with the accuracy of Command Line input. In this mode, AutoCAD displays the coordinates of the mouse position or the angle, length or other dimension that the current drawing will have if you click at that moment. It also allows you to enter values on the workspace, rather than in the Command Line. (You do, of course, type in exactly the same place as usual – i.e. through the keyboard – but this way you can keep your focus on the workspace.)

The drawing tools are used as normal, except that you now have an alternative way to input values. Have a little play, and see how it might help you in your work.

1 Click the **DYN** button in the Status bar to turn on Dynamic Input mode.

2 Select the Line tool, and start to draw a line. You will see a message by the cross-hair cursor, asking you to 'Specify first point'. Next to it are the coordinates of the point under the mouse. If you click, that's where the line will start.

3 If you want to set exact values, they can be typed in. The first coordinate (X) will be highlighted – to specify it, type a new value now. Press [**Tab**] to move to the Y coordinate, then type in its value. Press [**Enter**] when you have finished.

4 As you draw out the line, its length and angle will be displayed. Click to locate the next point, or type in the values to set its dimensions. The length will be highlighted, which means that it can be replaced by a typed value. Press [**Tab**] to move the highlight to the angle value if you want to enter this.

Saving and closing files

Your work is precious and computers are not 100% reliable! Save your drawings early and save them often, so that if your machine crashes or is inadvertently turned off, a recent copy of the file is available.

It only takes a few moments to save a drawing the first time. Resaving is even quicker – and you can have backup copies saved automatically.

To save a file for the first time:

1 Open the **File** menu and select **Save...** to open the **Save Drawing As** dialog box.

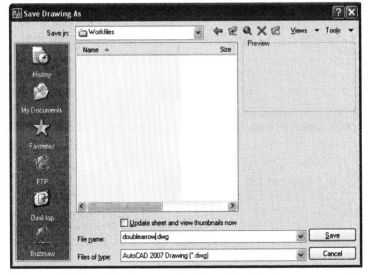

Figure 1.18 Saving a file – leave the **Files of type** at the default.

2 Check that the folder in the **Save in** slot is the right one. If not click the down arrow on the right of the box to select a higher level folder, or pick a subfolder from the main display.

3 Give the file a meaningful file name.

4 Click **Save**.

To resave a file:

◆ Select **Save** from the **File** menu, or click the **Save** button.

To use automatic saving:

1 Open the **Tools** menu and select **Options...**

2 Click on the **Open and Save** tab to open that panel.

3 In the **File Safety Precautions** area, tick the **Automatic save** checkbox and set the **Minutes between saves** value – something between 10 and 30 minutes will generally do.

4 Tick **Create backup copy with each save** if you want the extra security.

Figure 1.19 Setting the save options.

5 Tick **Full-time CRC validation** if you are having problems saving files successfully – this will check that an uncorrupted copy is stored on the disk.

6 Switch to the **Files** tab and double-click on the **Automatic Save File Location** entry to find out where the files are stored.

7 Click **OK** to close the **Options** dialog box.

Opening files

You can have any number of files open at once in AutoCAD – which can be very useful as it means that you can easily copy material from one to another.

1 Open the **File** menu and select **Open...**

2 At the **Select File** dialog box, browse through to the folder in the **Look in** slot.

3 Click on a file and look at its preview to check that it is the right one.

4 Click **Open**.

Figure 1.20 Opening a file. The Preview can help to identify files.

To move between open files:

◆ Open the **Window** menu and select the name of the file.

To close files:

◆ Open the **File** menu and select **Close**. If the file has not been saved recently, you will be prompted to save it.

Exercises

1 Use the Line tool to draw these three objects. Use snap to grid for the first, simple coordinates for the second and relative coordinates for the third.

(1) 120,160; 280,160; 280,140; 120,140; 120,160

(2) 50,150; 120,200; 120,100; 50,150

(3) 280,200; @70,-50; @-70,-50; @0,100

What shape do you have? These lines should have produced a large double-headed arrow.

2 Use polar coordinates to draw these two objects.

(1) 10,100; @25<45; @50<0; @25<315; @50<270; @25<180; @25<0; @25<315; @50<270; @25<225; @50<180; @25<135.

(2) 200,200; @25<135; @50<180; @25<225; @137<270; @25<315; @50<0; @25<45; @50<90; @25<135; @67<180.

You should have the digits 3 and 6. Draw 5 to the same scale with its top right corner at 320,300.

3 If you have not already done so, explore the sample files – find them in the Program Files/AutoCAD2007/Sample folder.

Summary

* The AutoCAD window has a Command Line window below the main working space.

* There are over 30 toolbars. These can be turned on and off as required, and docked at the top or sides of the window, or left floating anywhere on screen.

* Palettes are an convenient alternative to toolbars for accessing sets of tools.

* The right mouse button can be set to act as an [Enter] keypress. If the mouse has a wheel, it can be used for zooming and panning around the working space.

* The drawing is created in model space, but is arranged for printed output in paper space.

* You can zoom in and out with the Zoom tools.

* You can pick coordinates with the mouse – Snap and Object Snap will enable you to do this more accurately.

* Coordinates can be typed into the Command Line, as simple, relative or polar coordinates.

* The Line tool is used for drawing straight lines. A series of lines can be drawn at one time, with the end of one being the start of the next.

* Lines can be selected individually, or in groups. Once selected they can be edited or deleted.

* Drawing files should be saved regularly to guard against loss of work.

* When opening files, the preview can help to identify them.

02

the drawing tools

In this chapter you will learn:

- about the drawing tools
- how to set options
- how to select and edit objects

The Draw menu and the toolbar

The first thing you should learn about the drawing tools is that the toolbar only holds a selection of them. For the full set, you have to use the Draw menu, or the Command window.

The second thing to note is that several of the tools have options which give you an extra level of control over the shape or appearance of the object.

The Draw toolbar

Not all of the Draw tools are covered here. We used the Line tool in Chapter 1; we will look at the other drawing tools in Chapter 3, Hatch and Gradient in Chapter 5, and Table and Multiline text in Chapter 6. The Revision Cloud can be used to draw scalloped outlines around areas, and I will leave you to experiment with that.

Rectangles

The Rectangle tool is one of the simplest to use.

1 Click the **Rectangle** tool ⧈.

2 Pick or type the coordinates of a corner.

3 Drag and pick at the opposite corner, or type its coordinates.

Rectangles are always drawn parallel to the axes. If you want one at an angle, rotate it afterwards (see page 57).

* A rectangle can be drawn square, but it may be easier to create squares using the **Polygon** tool.

Figure 2.1 Drawing a simple rectangle.

Rectangle options

When the command first starts – before the first point has been defined – you are offered these options:

*   **Chamfer** cuts off the corner at an angle. It takes two chamfer distances. If these are the same, the angle is 45°. If they are different, the effect is as shown below.

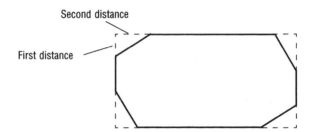

• **Elevation** is the distance *above* the drawing surface. Most tools draw flat on the surface unless you type in the z coordinates. The effect is, of course, only visible in 3D views.

• **Fillet** gives rounded corners. You set the radius of the arc.

• **Thickness** adds a third dimension to the rectangle, so that the lines become blocks. This is only visible in 3D views.

• **Width** sets the width of the line. The default is 0, which shows as a hairline on the drawing.

After specifying the first point, you can use the **Dimension** option to define the rectangle by its length and width, rather than giving the coordinates of the opposite corner.

The options are all set in much the same way:

1 Type the first letter of the name, e.g. this selects Chamfer:

Specify first corner point or
[Chamfer/Elevation/Fillet/Thickness/Width]: c

2 Type a value or press **[Enter]** to accept the offered default, e.g. after selecting the Chamfer option:

Specify first chamfer distance for rectangles<0.000>:5
Specify second chamfer distance for rectangles<5.000>:10

AutoCAD options

When you are setting an option, AutoCAD will offer you the current value – if this is what you want, press [Enter] to accept it. Note carefully that option values remain set in a drawing until changed. If you draw a rectangle at an elevation of 50, the next one will be up there unless you reset the elevation.

Examples

The four rectangles in Figure 2.2 are all basically the same size, but have these different options set.

1 Chamfer, first distance 20, second distance 10.

2 Elevation, 40 and Width, 5.

3 Thickness, 50.

4 Fillet, radius 20 and Thickness, 25

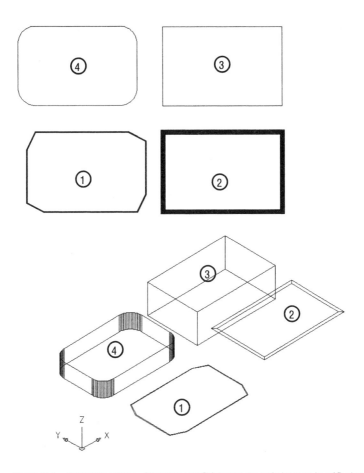

Figure 2.2 Rectangle options. Elevation and Thickness can only be seen in a 3D view – the lower image is seen in the **View > 3D Views > SW Isometric** display.

Point and type

Combine the visual display of drawing with a mouse or other pointing device and the accuracy of typed coordinates. Use the mouse to draw your lines so that you can see the image develop, but instead of picking the endpoints, type the coordinates using the values in the Status bar as a guide.

Circles

The **Circle** tool is another very simple one.

1 Click the **Circle** tool .

2 Pick or type the centre coordinates.

3 Type or drag and pick to set the radius.

There are several variations, which you can see best if you start the command from the **Draw** menu.

Point to **Circle** and you will offered six ways to define one:

* **Center, Radius** works the same way as the **Circle** tool.

* **Center, Diameter** is almost identical, though less intuitive to draw as the diameter indicator extends beyond the circle.

The other four variations allow you to construct circles that meet up with two or more objects.

* With the **2 Points** option, you pick or type two points which will form the ends of a diameter.

* With **3 Points,** you specify any three points that the circle must touch.

* With **Tan, Tan, Radius** you specify two lines that the circle must touch without intersecting (i.e. the tangent points) and the radius of the circle.

* For the **Tan, Tan, Tan** option you need to specify three tangent points for the circle.

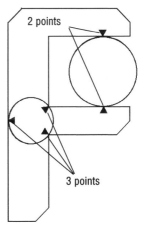

Figure 2.3 Drawing circles using the 2 points and 3 points methods.

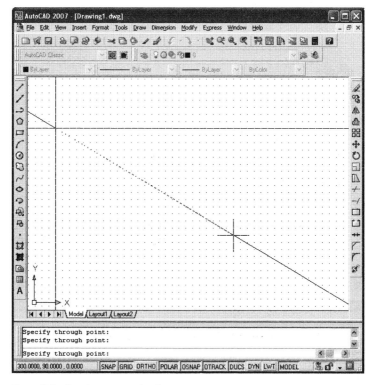

Construction lines

Construction lines can help you to place and align objects. The lines extend the full width of the working space – and beyond – and are defined by specifying two points on the line. If several lines are drawn at one time, they all pass through the first point.

1 Click the **Construction line** tool ⁄.

2 Pick or type the coordinates to specify the first point.

3 Specify the second point.

4 Repeat **3** to define other lines passing through the first point.

5 Press [**Enter**] to end.

6 Start again from **1** to draw additional lines that do not pass through the first point.

Figure 2.4 Drawing construction lines.

Polygons

A polygon is a shape with any number of equal sides. You can use the Polygon tool to create squares, triangles, pentagons, hexagons or whatever – any regular shape of up to 1024 sides!

Polygons can be defined in three ways:

* By the position and size of one edge – as all the other edges will be the same length this is enough to define the polygon.

* By the centre and the radius of a circle that it could be circumscribed around – i.e. the distance to the midpoint of an edge.

* By the centre and the radius of the circle that it could be inscribed in – i.e. the distance to a vertex.

Circumscribed

Inscribed

To define a polygon by an edge:

1 Click the **Polygon** tool.

2 Type the number of sides required.

3 Type 'E' to select Edge mode.

4 Specify the point at one end of an edge.

5 Drag to draw the line – the polygon, based on this, will take shape. Pick or type the coordinates to specify the endpoint.

To define a polygon by its centre and radius:

1 Click the **Polygon** tool and type the number of sides.

2 Specify the centre point.

3 Type 'I' to select Inscribed, or 'C' for Circumscribed mode.

4 Type the radius.

Or

5 Use the mouse to drag the polygon to size and rotate it as required, clicking when it is in the right position.

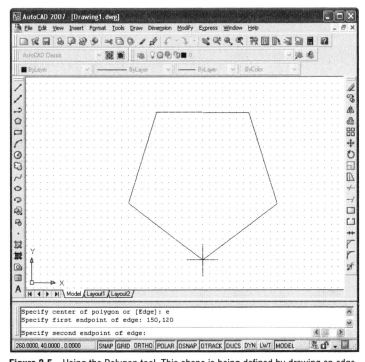

Figure 2.5 Using the Polygon tool. This shape is being defined by drawing an edge.

Arcs

There are a dozen ways to draw an arc. The one linked to the **Arc** tool creates an arc from the start, end and another point anywhere else on the arc. The arc will be drawn clockwise or anticlockwise, depending upon the position of the points. In all the other modes the arcs are drawn *anticlockwise* – keep this in mind when specifying start or end points.

To draw an arc from three points:

1 Click the **Arc** tool.

2 Specify the start point.

3 Specify another point anywhere on the arc – a straight line will (temporarily) link it to the start point.

4 Specify the end point.

Start

Second point

End

The **Arc** command variations use different combinations of the seven points or measurements shown here, e.g. Start, Centre and End, or Start, End and Angle. Note that only three of these values – and it can be any three – are needed to define an arc.

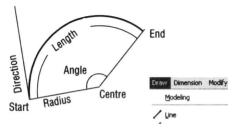

End

Length

Direction

Angle

Start   Radius   Centre

• The *direction* is that of the tangent to the arc at the start point.

To draw an Arc:

1 Open the **Draw** menu and point to **Arc**.

2 Select the Arc option that best fits with the drawing that you have developed to that stage.

3 Type the values or pick the coordinates to define the points, angle or length in the appropriate order.

Continuation lines

If you want to draw a tangent which continues directly on from the end of the arc, there is a simple way to do this:

1 Select the Line tool and press [Enter] to accept the end of the arc as the start point for the line.

2 Specify the length of the line only – AutoCAD will automatically set it to the arc's end angle.

Splines

This draws a continuous line with multiple curves. The line is defined largely by the points on the cusps of the curves. The curves at the start and end are defined separately afterwards.

To draw a spline:

1 Click on the **Spline** tool 〰.

2 Click or type the coordinates to specify the start point.

3 Specify the points to locate the curves along the line.

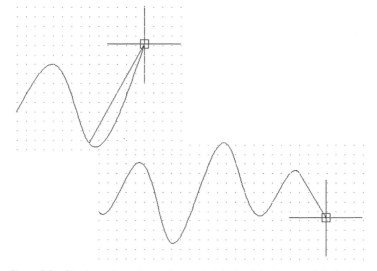

Figure 2.6 Drawing splines. As you draw, a straight line links the cross-hairs back to the previous point.

4 Press [**Enter**] at the end.

5 A straight line will appear, connecting to the start point. Move this to form the first curve. Repeat for the end curve.

Ellipses

An ellipse has two axes that cross at right angles. The shape is defined by the length of those axes, and their angle to the grid.

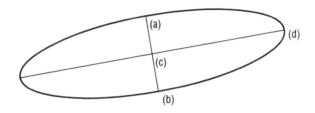

To define an ellipse:

1 Click on the **Ellipse** tool .

2 Specify the position of the startpoint of an axis (a).

3 Drag and pick or type the coordinates to set the length and angle of the axis (b).

4 Specify the length of the other axis, from the centre (c) to the edge (d) – its angle will be 90 degrees to the first.

The ⬯ tool is the same as the **Draw > Ellipse > Axis, End** option. The **Draw** menu also has an **Ellipse > Center** option. In this, the first point to be defined is the centre, and both axes are defined by specifying their length from the centre.

Ellipse arcs

An ellipse arc is defined by first creating an ellipse, then marking the start and end angles of the arc within it. When setting these, remember that arcs are drawn anticlockwise.

1 Click on the **Ellipse Arc** tool 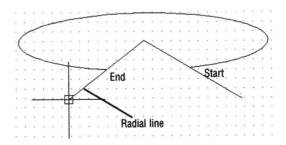.

2 Draw an ellipse as shown above.

3 A radial line will appear. Type the start angle, or swing the radial line around the centre to point to the start, then click to pick the angle.

4 Type the angle or swing the line and pick the end angle.

Points

Points are used to act as snap points to help in the construction of other objects. Their screen appearance depends upon the point style, and can be highly visible – which you may need when using them as guides – or totally invisible – so they don't intrude on the finished drawing. The default style is a single pixel.

Figure 2.7 An arc being drawn using points as guides.

To place points:

1 Click the **Point** tool .

2 Type or pick its coordinates.

3 Repeat 2 to place more points as required.

4 Press [Escape] or select another tool to end.

To set the point style:

1 Open the **Format** menu and select **Point Style…**

2 Select a style.

3 If required, set the size, either as relative to the screen or in absolute units.

4 Click **OK**.

• The style will be applied to any existing points and to all that you draw from that time. Come back and change the style later to make the points more or less visible.

Polylines

The Polyline tool is used in basically the same way as the Line tool, but there are several differences in the result. The first is that even when used in a continuous sequence, Line-drawn lines are separate objects, but Polyline-drawn lines form a single object – clicking anywhere on a polyline selects the whole set. A polyline does not have to end back at the startpoint, but if it does, this creates a closed object which can be filled (Chapter 5).

The other differences arise from the greater flexibility of polylines. A polyline can be a straight line or an arc, and it can be of any thickness – and the thickness can taper from one end to the other. As a result, you can produce more or less any shape with the Polyline – we'll start with something simple, then go on to explore it.

1 Click the **Polyline** tool .

2 Click to pick the start of the first line or type the coordinates.

3 Drag and pick to draw the line, or type the coordinates of the endpoint. Repeat as necessary.

4 Press [Enter] (or right-click) to end.

Figure 2.8 A simple polyline under construction.

Polyline options

Polyline has a number of options which can be selected when you see the prompt:

Specify next point or [Arc/Close/Halfwidth/Length/Undo/Width]

Arc: draws an arc, instead of a straight line. Unless you specify otherwise, the arc will be such that the previous line would meet it at a tangent. In practice, this means that you can use it to draw rounded corners and ends without further specification.

In arc-drawing mode, there are the additional options: **Angle, Center, Direction, Line, Radius, Second point** and **End point.**

Line reverts to line-drawing mode; the rest are used for specifying the position and angle of the arc. The simplest are **Direction,** which sets the tangent direction – you can see this in examples 3 and 4 in Figure 2.9 – and **Second point** and **End point,** which are used as they are with the **Arc** tool.

Close: draws a line from the last endpoint to the start of the polyline, creating a closed shape. This can be filled (Chapter 5).

Halfwidth: is – literally – half the width of the line. Use it in exactly the same way as Width (but at half the value!).

Length: draws a straight line of the given length, continuing at the same angle as the previous line or as a tangent from an arc.

Undo: undoes the last command within the polyline. This is very useful, as things can go wrong with this complex feature, and it would be a shame to have to start again from scratch because of one error.

Width: the start and end widths are set separately, and if they are different, the line's thickness will smoothly taper from one to the other over its length.

To set polyline options:

1 Type the first (and sometimes the second) letter of the name, e.g. this selects Arc drawing mode, then the Center option:

Specify next point or [Arc/Halfwidth/Length/Undo/Width]: A
Specify endpoint of arc or [Angle/CEnter/Direction/Halfwidth/
    Line/Radius/Second pt/Undo/Width]: CE

2 Type a value or press [**Enter**] to accept the offered default, e.g. after selecting the Width option:

Specify starting width <1.000>: 5
Specify ending width <5.000>: 25

Figure 2.9 Examples of polylines.

The polylines in Figure 2.9 were produced by the following command sequences:

1 Start point: 50,50

Option: Width, Starting 20, Ending 1

Second point, @100,0 [Enter]

2 Start point: 50,120
Second point: 200,120
Option: Arc
Next point: 200,80
Option: Line
Next point: 50,80
Option: Arc
Next point: 50,120 Close

3 Start point: 50,140
Option: Width, Starting 2, Ending 2
Next point: 100,140
Option: Arc
Option: Direction, 90
Next point: 170,140
Option: Line
Next point: 220,140

4 Start point: 200,200
Option: Width, Starting 20, Ending 5
Option: Arc
Option: Direction, 105
Next point: 80,210
Option: Width, Starting 40, Ending 0
Option: Line
Next point: 50,170

Selecting and editing objects

To select a single object:

◆ Click on one of its lines.

To select several objects close to each other:

◆ Drag an outline to enclose all or touch on the objects.

To select scattered objects:

◆ Hold [**Shift**] and click on each of the objects in turn.

A selected object is shown in dashed lines with grips (blue squares) at each vertex. Circles and ellipses also have a handle at the centre.

To move an object:

• Click on any line – not a grip – and drag into position.

To delete an object:

• Select it and press [**Delete**] or click the **Eraser** .

Adjusting the shape

You can adjust the shape of an object by dragging its grips. The effect varies with the nature of the shape, and this may not be the best way to edit an object. In Chapter 3 we will look at the Modify tools, which can be used to manipulate objects in different ways; and in Chapter 4 you will meet the Properties panel, where you can define the positions of vertices accurately.

To move a vertex (distorting the shape):

1 Drag on the grip. The new position of the vertex and the length and angles of the lines joining at it will be shown.

2 Release the mouse when you are happy with the shape.

To change the width or length of a rectangle:

1 Hold down [**Shift**].

2 Click on the vertices at the opposite ends of a side.

3 Drag on either vertex to move the line smoothly in or out. It will remain at right angles to the adjacent sides.

4 Release the button to fix the new width/length.

- You can use the same technique to move any number of vertices of a polygon or polyline at once. The vertices will all move in the same direction and angle. You must hold [Shift] before you start to select the vertices.

To change the size of a circle:

1 Click on one of the quadrant grips (those on the perimeter).

2 Drag in or out to set the size – the circle will not be distorted.

3 Release the button when the circle is the right size.

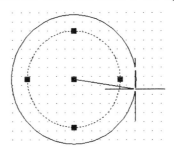

To change the shape of an ellipse:

1 Click on the grip at the end of one of the axes.

2 Drag in or out to change its length (and the shape of the ellipse).

3 Release the button when the axis is the right length.

4 Repeat for the other axis if required.

Exercises

1 Use the Rectangle and Circle tools to draw this pattern.

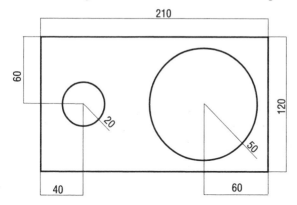

2 Use the Rectangle tool to draw the next object. The outside rectangle has a fillet of 20. Remember to reset the fillet to 0 before starting to draw the inside rectangle.

3 Use the Polygon and Line tools to draw the next design. (Tip: use object snap and polar coordinates to define the lines that radiate out from the polygon.)

4 Construct this shape using the Polyline tool – it will actually take several polylines to create the whole outline.

Summary

+ Most drawing tools can be selected from the Draw toolbar. The Draw menu has all of these and more.

+ Rectangles are defined by any two opposite corners.

+ Circles can be drawn by giving the centre and radius, or by specifying points that they must intersect or meet.

+ Construction lines can be added to help align objects.

+ Polygons can have up to 1024 sides. They can be defined by an edge, or by the position and size of their circles.

+ There are a dozen ways to draw an arc!

+ A spline is a curved line. It is defined by the cusps of its curves and the tangents of its ends.

+ An ellipse has two axes at right angles to each other, and is defined by the length of those axes.

+ To create an ellipse arc, you first draw an ellipse, then mark the start and end angles of the arc.

+ Points can be used to help to draw other objects.

+ A polyline has a number of lines, which are treated as a single unit. The command has several options.

+ You can adjust the shape and size of objects by dragging on the grips.

03 modifying objects

In this chapter you will learn:

- about the modify tools
- how to copy, move and rotate objects
- how to trim or extend lines
- how to chamfer and fillet angles

The Modify toolbar

The Modify toolbar contains all key tools you need for manipulating objects. Many of them work in similar ways, so that once you have mastered one tool, the next is easier to get to grips with. Notice in particular how objects are selected, and the use of a base point. Learn about these first with the Erase and Copy tools.

Rotate   Extend   Chamfer

Mirror   Move   Trim   Join   Fillet

Erase   Array   Stretch   Break   Explode

Copy   Offset   Scale   Break at point

Erase

This is the simplest of the Modify tools.

1 Select the objects you want to remove.

2 Click the **Erase** tool ✎.

Or

1 Click the **Erase** tool ✎.

2 Select the objects you want to remove.

3 Press **[Enter]** or right-click to tell AutoCAD that you have finished selecting objects.

Selecting objects for modifying

Objects can be selected before or after clicking the tool. It is simplest to select them first. If you start the tool first, AutoCAD goes into a 'select object' mode. You can then select objects by dragging over them or [Shift]-clicking, or a combination of both – but AutoCAD will stay in its 'select object' mode until you press [Enter] to signal that you have got them all. Watch out for this. If you are used to working in other Windows applications, it does not feel intuitive.

Copy

The standard Windows Copy and Paste technique works perfectly well, but it is worth knowing about the Copy command as it can give you better control when you place the copies.

After selecting the objects, you must specify a base point. The copy is then located by giving the position of its base point. This allows very accurate positioning.

By default, only one copy is made at a time. If several are wanted, switch on the multiple option at the start of the command.

Figure 3.1 Making a copy – a line joins the base points of the original (dotted outline) and the copy while it is being placed. Note that the Modify menu has a few more commands than the toolbar.

To copy:

1 Select the object(s).

2 Click the **Copy** tool .

Or

♦ Click the **Copy** tool, select the objects and press **[Enter]**.

3 If multiple copies are needed, type 'M' in the Command Line.

4 Pick a base point in or near the objects.

5 Pick where you want to place the base point of the copy.

6 In Multiple mode, place the other copies then press **[Enter]**.

Polar: 39.5944 < 270°

Figure 3.2 Making multiple copies. Here polar tracking has been turned on (press [F10] to toggle it on or off) to show when the copy is at a right angle to the original.

Mirror

The Mirror tool produces a mirror image, allowing you to create a symmetrical object by drawing only half of it – or even a smaller fraction. You place the mirror line by picking two points on it – the line will swivel after the first point has been set, and you will be able to see how the reflection will look and where it will appear. Picking the second point fixes the line and creates the new drawing – the original can be kept or removed as desired.

To create a mirror image:

1 Select the object(s).

2 Click the **Mirror** tool.

Or

◆ Click the **Mirror** tool 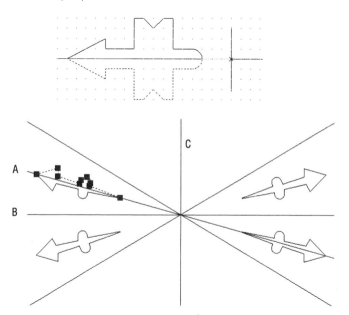, select the objects and press **[Enter]**.

3 Pick the coordinates of one point on the mirror line.

4 Pick the second point to fix the line.

5 The Command Line will prompt:

Delete source objects? [Yes/No] <N> :

Type 'Y' to delete the object, or press **[Enter]** to accept the default (No).

Figure 3.3 Mirrored objects. Top: a reflection in the horizontal. Bottom: a multiple image created by mirroring the polyline first in line A, then in line B, then in line C.

Offset

Offset creates copies of an outline within or outside the source shape. It is unusual in that you cannot select an object first – you must start with the tool (or command) and specify the offset distance before selecting the object.

1 Select the **Offset** tool .

2 Type the offset distance into the Command Line.

3 Click on the source object.

4 Click inside or outside of the object to tell AutoCAD whether to make an inner or outer offset.

5 Repeat step **4** to create more offsets of the same object, or go back to step **3** to select a new object.

6 Press [**Enter**] or right-click to end.

Figure 3.4   Clicking at this point would create an offset inside the original shape.

Array

This creates a regularly spaced array of copies of an object. The array can be a rectangular grid or a polar pattern, radiating around a central point.

To create a rectangular array:

1 Select the object(s).

2 Click the **Array** tool.

Or

• Click the **Array** tool, select the objects and press [**Enter**].

3 Select the **Rectangular Array** option at the top of the **Array** dialog box.

4 Set the number of **Rows** and **Columns**.

5 Enter the **Row** and **Column offsets** – the distance between the same points on two copies.

6 The **Angle of array** tilts the array from the horizontal. Set a value if required.

7 Click **OK**.

Figure 3.5 The array produced by the settings in the dialog box, based on the selected 'window frame' object.

To create a polar array:

1 Start as for a rectangular array, but select the **Polar Array** option in the **Array** dialog box.

2 Type the **Center point** coordinates, or click 🔣 and pick the point.

3 Set the **Total number of items** and the **Angle to fill**.

4 Tick or clear the **Rotate items as copied** checkbox on the bottom left, as required.

5 Click **OK**.

Figure 3.6 An example of a polar array.

Move

You can move an object by dragging. The main advantage of the Move tool is its greater accuracy. It also avoids the possibility of distorting an object by dragging on a handle, instead of a line.

1 Select the object(s).

2 Click the **Move** tool ⊹.

Or

• Click the **Move** tool ⊹, select the objects and press **[Enter]**.

3 Pick a base point in or near the objects.

4 Type the coordinates or pick where you want to move the base point to.

Figure 3.7 Moving an object.

Rotate

An object can be rotated about a point within its shape or outside of it.

1 Select the object(s).

2 Click the **Rotate** tool ⟳.

Or

♦ Click the **Rotate** tool ⟳, select the objects and press [**Enter**].

3 Type the coordinates or pick the point to rotate around.

4 Type the angle, or use the mouse to rotate the object.

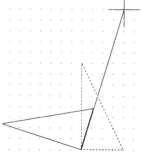

Figure 3.8 You can rotating an object by dragging the guide line.

Scale

Scaling makes an object uniformly larger or smaller. It works by changing all the coordinates by the same factor and in relation to a given point. You can visualize it as projecting a shadow, and the size of a shadow depends upon the relative positions of the object and the light source.

1 Select the object(s).

2 Click the **Scale** tool ▢.

Or

• Click the **Scale** tool ▣, select the objects and press [**Enter**].

3 Pick a base point within the object to change its size without moving it, or outside to change the size and position.

4 Type the scale factor in at the Command Line – the values are usually too small to set accurately with a mouse.

Figure 3.9 Scaling changes the size and position of an object relative to a given point. This shows a scale factor of 2.

Stretch

This will take part of an object and move it in relation to the rest to stretch – or shrink – the overall shape. You could do the same job by selecting the handles at one end and dragging them, but this is a little simpler.

As with the **Offset** command, you must start **Stretch** before you select the objects. Selection is done using a 'crossing window' – a dotted rectangle that appears when you drag across the screen. Any object inside or touched by this window is selected.

1 Select the **Stretch** tool ▣.

2 Click to fix one corner of the crossing window.

3 Drag the window over the objects you want to select, and click to fix its other corner.

4 Press [Enter] to end the select object routine.

5 Type the coordinates or pick a point in the selected area.

6 Type the new coordinates or drag the point to where you want to stretch it.

Figure 3.10 Using Stretch to lengthen a shape.

Trim and Extend

Rather than draw exactly the right shape or length of lines, it is sometimes simpler to draw to the approximate length or shape, and then trim off the excess or extend lines to make an exact fit.

You can trim to where a line meets an existing line, or add new lines to act as the 'cutting edge'. Similarly, when extending lines, an existing or a temporary line can act as the boundary edge.

To trim a line or shape:

1 If necessary, draw the cutting edge lines.

2 Click the **Trim** tool ⧊.

3 Select the lines to act as the cutting edge, then press [Enter].

4 Click on the lines or shapes where they project beyond the cutting edge.

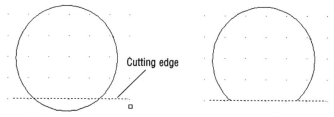

Figure 3.11 Trimming a shape.

5 Repeat to trim other lines or shapes and press [**Enter**] to end.

6 If the cutting edge line has no other purpose, delete it.

To extend lines:

1 If necessary, draw the boundary edge lines.

2 Click the **Extend** tool ⊣.

3 Select the lines to act as the boundary edge and press [**Enter**].

4 Click on the lines to extend to meet the boundary edge.

5 Repeat to trim other lines or shapes. Press [**Enter**] to end.

6 If the boundary edge line has no other purpose, delete it.

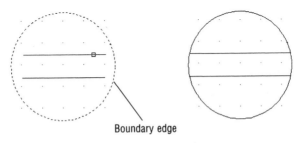

Boundary edge

Figure 3.12 Extending lines to meet a boundary edge.

Break

There are two versions of this tool. **Break** cuts a section out of a line or shape – use it for creating openings in solid outlines or as an alternative to **Trim**. **Break at point** cuts through a line or a shape, creating two lines though the ends still meet – use it to subdivide lines so that the sections can be manipulated separately or as an alternative to **Explode** (see page 64) to cut one line out of a polygon or polyline.

You must select the tool first in both versions.

To break a line:

1 Select the **Break** tool ▭.

2 Click on the line at the point where you want to break it – this selects the line and the break point.

3 Click where you want the second break point.

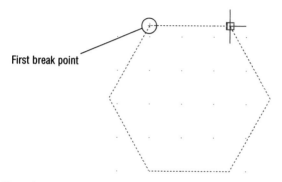

First break point

Figure 3.13 Setting the second break point in a selected shape. The line between these points will then be removed.

To break at a point:

1 Select the **Break at point** tool ⬛.

2 Click on the line or shape to select it.

3 Click where you want the break point.

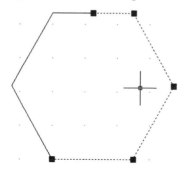

Figure 3.14 The shape will appear to be unchanged after setting a break point, but if you click on it, you will see that only one part will be selected.

Join

Join will put back together a line, arc, circle, polyline or spline that has been broken apart. It can also be used to join objects that were drawn separately in the first place – but only if they could have been drawn as one. You can, for example, only join two lines if one is a direct continuation of the other.

Chamfer

We met chamfer earlier as an option when drawing rectangles. The Chamfer tool does a similar job – it cuts off a corner at an angle. It works on a vertex of any shape or on any pair of lines that can intersect – though they do not have to actually meet or cross. The chamfer angle is determined by the distances along the first and second lines from the point of intersection – and which line is first or second depends on the order in which you select them.

For example, to chamfer this corner, we would set up the first chamfer distances as 5 and the second as 10, then select A as the first line and B as the second.

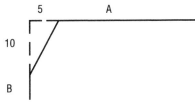

- The chamfer option on a rectangle applies to all four corners. The chamfer tool normally only cuts one corner at a time. The Multiple option will let you apply the same cut successively to any number of corners. The Polyline option will apply the current chamfer settings to every angle in a polyline object.

1 Click the **Chamfer** tool .

2 The current chamfer distances will be shown in the Command Line. If these are OK, go to step **5**.

3 If you want to chamfer several corners, type 'U' to turn on the Multiple option.

4 Type 'D' to select the Distance option.

5 Enter the first then the second chamfer distances.

```
(TRIM mode) Current chamfer Dist1 = 10.0000, Dist2 = 5.0000
Select first line or [Polyline/Distance/Angle/Trim/Method/mUltiple]: d
Specify first chamfer distance <10.0000>: 5
Specify second chamfer distance <5.0000>:
```

6 Select the line to apply the first chamfer distance to.

7 Select the second line.

8 Repeat steps **6** and **7** for other corners if in Multiple mode.

Fillet

This is similar to but simpler than **Chamfer**. It will round off any corner, or draw an arc to join a pair of lines that intersect or could intersect if extended.

◆ If the lines do not meet, and the radius of the fillet will not produce an arc big enough to join them, the lines will be extended to connect to the arc.

◆ If the lines intersect, the parts of the lines beyond the fillet arc will normally be trimmed. If you want to retain them, turn the Trim option off.

◆ The Multiple and Polyline options are the same as in **Chamfer**.

1 Click the **Fillet** tool.

2 Check the current settings.

3 Type 'R' then the value to change the Radius.

4 Type 'T', then the setting if you want to change the Trim mode.

5 Type 'U' if you want to turn on the Multiple option.

6 Select the two lines to fillet – the order is irrelevant.

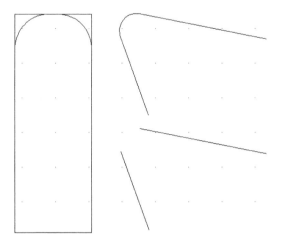

Figure 3.15 Using Fillet – applied to two corners of a rectangle with the Trim option off (left); two lines joined by a fillet, before (below right) and after (top right).

Explode

This will break up a polyline, polygon or rectangle into its component lines. Use it if you need to delete or change the properties of one line in a compound object without affecting the rest.

It can also be used to break up blocks (see Chapter 9) into their components.

1 Select the object(s).

2 Click the **Explode** tool 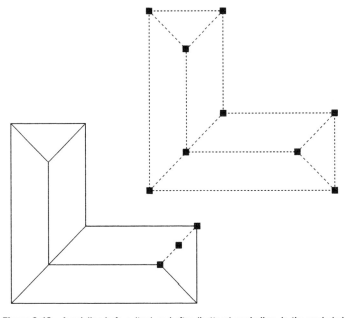.

Or

◆ Click the **Explode** tool, select the objects and press [**Enter**].

An explosion is irreversible! If you need to reassemble the lines into a unit so that it can be handled more conveniently, you can make them into a block – which we will look at in Chapter 9.

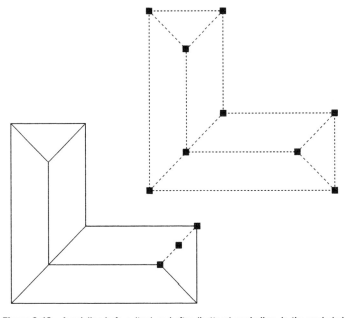

Figure 3.16 A polyline before (top) and after (bottom) exploding. In the exploded drawing, it is possible to select – and edit – one line without affecting the rest.

Exercises

1 Draw a right-angled triangle, 80 units high by 40 wide. Mirror it along its hypotenuse, keeping the original. Select and rotate the two triangles together, picking the lower end of the hypotenuse as the base point, to produce the 'arrowhead' effect shown here.

2 Draw a circle of radius 50 units. Using the Offset tool, create four more circles within it, each 10 units smaller than the next. Draw a square of 70 units, with its top left corner at the centre of the circles. Use this as a cutting edge to trim the lower right quadrants from the circle, to produce this image.

3 Draw a house image, based on a rectangle of 80 by 60 units, with a roof, windows and a door. Use the Scale tool to reduce it to half size. Create eight copies of it with a polar array to produce something like this.

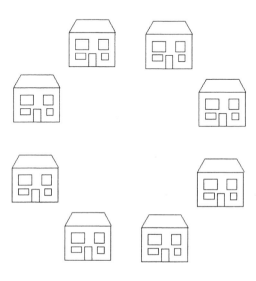

Summary

♦ The main tools for editing and manipulating objects can be found on the Modify toolbar.

♦ With most modify tools, you can either select the objects before the tool, or vice versa.

♦ Press [Delete] or use the Erase tool to remove unwanted objects.

♦ The Copy tool gives you better control over the placing of copies than the standard Windows Copy and Paste.

♦ An object can be reflected in any mirror plane.

♦ The Offset tool allows you to create copies of a shape within or outside the original.

♦ A whole set of copies can be created at once with the Array tool. They can be arranged in a rectangluar or polar pattern.

♦ An object can be rotated around any point, within or beyond its boundaries.

♦ Scaling changes the size and position of an object in relation to a base point.

♦ The stretch routine allows you to make part of an object longer, without affecting the rest.

♦ Lines can be cut to length with the Trim tool, or extended to intersect a boundary. They can also be broken at a point, or by removing a section.

♦ Broken – or separate but continuous – lines, arcs and polylines can be joined.

♦ The point of an intersection can be chamfered or filleted.

♦ A polyline, rectangle, polygon or block can be exploded into its components.

04

properties

In this chapter you will learn:

- about the properties of lines and shapes
- how to format lines from the Properties toolbar options
- how to display and to use the Properties palette

The Properties toolbar

You can set the type, weight and colour of lines with the options in the drop-down lists on the **Properties** toolbar, and add to the range of available settings, change the defaults and adjust other aspects of these properties through the commands on the **Format** menu.

ByLayer and ByBlock

At the top of each of the line properties drop-down list are the options **ByLayer** and **ByBlock**. You can set the default colour, type and weight for each layer of a drawing – see Chapter 8 for more on layers. An object with its properties set to **ByLayer** takes the colour, type and weight of the layer settings, and so will change if the defaults are changed, and if copied or inserted into another drawing will take the properties of the layer into which it is placed.

The current settings in the Properties toolbar are applied to new objects as they are drawn. These may be different from the defaults for the layer. For example, if you defined the layer to draw lines in red, but then set the colour option to blue, subsequent new lines would be drawn in blue.

If you create a block with its properties set to **ByBlock**, when it is inserted into a new drawing, it will take its colour, type and weight from the current selection in the Properties toolbar, or the ByLayer defaults if the properties have not been individually set.

If you want an object or block to retain its properties when copied or inserted, each must be set individually and not using either ByLayer or ByBlock.

Lineweight

By default, lines are 0.01" (0.25mm) wide, but the lineweights can be anything from 0.0mm up to 2.11mm. By default, however, the thickness is not shown on screen. AutoCAD normally draws all lines one pixel wide, rather than showing them at their actual widths, as this allows the screen to be redrawn much faster – remember that the displayed width is relative to the zoom level, so there is quite a lot of extra processing involved. If required, you can turn on the lineweight display.

- On simple drawings, screen redrawing is not significantly slower when lineweights are displayed, but the more complex the drawing, the more you will notice the difference.

To control the lineweight display:

1 Open the **Format** menu and select **Lineweight...**

2 At the **Lineweight Settings** dialog box, tick (or clear) the **Display Lineweight** checkbox.

3 Set the **Adjust Display Scale** slider to the centre or towards the **Min** end – the lower it is, the faster the system can work.

4 Pick a new value from the **Lineweights** list to set the Current Lineweight, if required.

5 Pick a new value from the **Default** drop-down list if you want to set a different default value.

6 Click **OK**.

Figure 4.1 Changing the default value will change the weight of any existing lines that have not had their lineweight set. Changing the current lineweight only affects lines drawn from that point on.

To set the lineweight:

1 Select the object(s) to format.

2 Drop down the **Lineweights** list on the Properties toolbar.

3 Select a recently-used weight from the top of the list, or scroll down to select a new value.

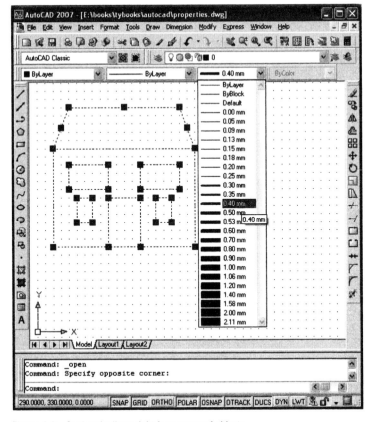

Figure 4.2 Setting the lineweight for a group of objects.

Linetype

If you want to indicate hidden lines or a different type of connection, e.g. wiring or plumbing in a building plan, you could use a different linetype.

Initially there are only three linetypes available from the drop-down list in the Properties toolbar, but more are easily added.

To add a linetype:

1 Open the Linetypes drop-down list and click **Other...**

Or

• Open the **Format** menu and select **Linetype...**

Figure 4.3 Loading a new line type. Note that as well as a range of dots and dashes, there are types for specific purposes.

2 At the **Linetype Manager** dialog box, click **Load...**

3 Scroll through the list and select a linetype.

4 If you want to add more types at the same time, hold down [Ctrl] and click on the others.

5 Click **OK** when you have selected your type(s).

6 Click **OK** to close the **Linetype Manager** dialog box.

To set the linetype:

1 Select the line(s) to be formatted.

2 Open the **Linetype** drop-down list.

3 If there is a suitable type, click on it.

Or

4 Click **Other...** to add a new line type to the list.

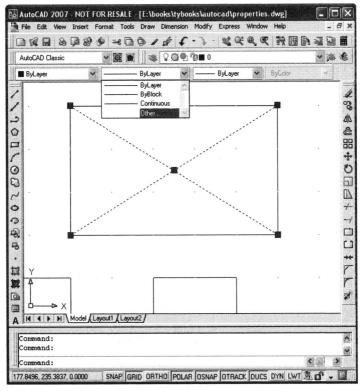

Figure 4.4 Setting the linetype.

Line colour

Line colour is also changed through a list on the Properties toolbar, and again there is initially a limited selection. If more or different colours are needed, they can be added via a very comprehensive routine.

To set the line colour:

1 Select the line(s) to be formatted.

2 Open the **Color** drop-down list.

3 If there is a suitable colour, click on it.

To add more colours to the list:

1 Click **Select Color...** at the bottom of the list.

Or

• Open the **Format** menu and select **Color...**

2 Go to a tab and select a colour.

• On the **Index Color** tab, select from AutoCAD's own set.

240 numbered colours

HSL or RGB?

Named colours

Greys

Drag to set the
shade brightness

Figure 4.5 The Index Color and True Color tabs.

- On the **True Color** tab, in the **Color model** slot at the top right, choose the **HSL** (Hue, Saturation, Luminance) or **RGB** (Red, Green, Blue), then set the values in the number fields or on the colour spectrum.

- On the **Color Books** tab, you can select industry standard colours from the Pantone or RAL ranges.

The Properties palette

The Properties palette can be used to view or change the colour, linetype, position, dimensions and other properties of objects.

The properties are grouped into sets, and for most objects there are three sets: *General*, *Geometry* and *Miscellaneous*, though what is in the palette depends upon what type of object – or types of objects – are selected at the time.

Almost all objects have the same *General* properties – colour, linetype, lineweight and the like. The *Geometry* properties vary according to how the object is drawn – a line is basically defined by its start and end coordinates; a circle by its centre and radius; an arc has the same properties as a circle, plus more to define its start and end. The simpler objects have no *Miscellaneous* properties.

If several objects are selected, the palette will only include those properties which they all share. But see for yourself...

The display of the properties in each set can be turned on and off by clicking the chevrons at the right of the title bars.

Figure 4.6 The Properties palette when no object is selected.

To open the Properties palette:

1 Click the 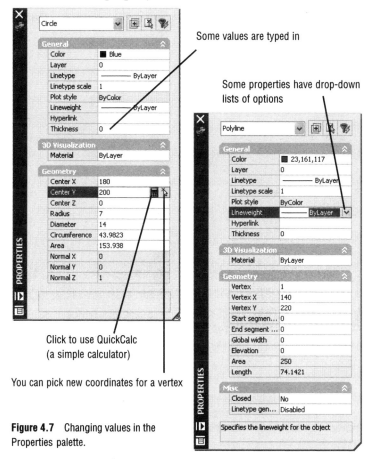 button on the Standard toolbar.

* When no object is selected, the palette shows the current settings for the drawing.

2 Click on an object in the drawing area to see its properties in the palette.

If a property is shown on a white background, it can be changed – exactly how depends on the nature of the property.

To change a property:

1 Click on the property to select it.

Some values are typed in

Some properties have drop-down lists of options

Click to use QuickCalc
(a simple calculator)

You can pick new coordinates for a vertex

Figure 4.7 Changing values in the Properties palette.

2 If it is a simple number, e.g. thickness, type in the new value.

3 If it is a coordinate, a pick arrow will appear on the right of the field. Click on this, then pick a new position for the vertex in the drawing area.

4 If a down arrow appears at the right of the field, click on this to drop down a list of options and select a value from there.

5 Polylines have a **Vertex** property – the number of the current vertex. This allows you to work round the vertices, and to view or adjust their coordinates. Use the arrows on the right of the field to change the number.

Figure 4.8 Changing the current vertex in a polyline.

Multiple selections

If you select several objects at once, you can set the same shared property for all of the objects in a single operation – and properties are set in the usual way.

The selected objects are grouped by type, and the whole lot grouped under the heading *All*. If you want to set the properties for the objects of one type, you can select that group from the drop-down list at the top of the palette.

Open the list...

...then pick a type

Figure 4.9 Working with multiple selections.

Auto-hide

The Properties panel is quite large, and can get in the way. The solution is to turn on Auto-hide. The palette will then shrink back to a title bar when the cursor is moved away from it, and re-open when the cursor is placed over the bar.

To turn Auto-hide on or off:

1 Click on the **Properties** icon ▤ at the bottom of the palette's title bar.

2 The **Auto-hide** option is a toggle switch – click it to turn it on (ticked), or off.

Or

• Click the **Auto-hide** icon ▣ on the title bar – this is also a toggle switch.

If the palette is not going to be wanted for a while, close it completely by clicking the **Close** button in the top right corner.

Exercises

1 Using the Polygon tool, draw a triangle starting at 100,100 with sides of 100 units. Set its lineweight to 0.30mm and its colour to green, by selecting from the drop-down lists.

2 Draw a square, starting at 100,0 with sides of 100 units. Change its linetype to short dashes and its colour to blue.

3 Draw a circle, centred at 150,50 with a radius of 50. Set its lineweight to 1.00mm and its colour to red.

4 Use the Offset tool to draw a second circle within the first, 25 units inside the line.

5 Open the Properties palette for the triangle. Redefine its top vertex 50 units higher, making it taller.

6 Using the Properties palette, change the square's line to solid, 0.5mm and its colour to magenta.

7 Using the Properties palette, change the centre of the larger circle to 150,150.

8 Select both circles and change their colour to black, using the Properties palette.

Summary

+ You can set the type, weight and colour of lines using the drop-down lists on the Properties toolbar.

+ Default properties can be set ByBlock or ByLayer.

+ Lineweights can be anything from 0.0mm (hairline) up to 2.11mm.

+ There are at first only three options in the linetypes drop-down list, but more can be added easily.

+ There is a limited choice of colours on the Properties toolbar, but an unlimited choice in the Select Color dialog box.

+ The Properties palette can be used to view or change the colour, line type, position, dimensions and other properties of objects.

05

fills and hatches

In this chapter you will learn:

- how to define and apply a hatch
- how hatches can be modifed and edited
- how to define and apply a gradient fill

Hatching

Any closed shapes – rectangles, circles, ellipses, polygons and closed polylines – can be filled with a hatch pattern or texture, or with solid or shaded colour.

Shapes may have other shapes within them, creating 'islands' – and they may be nested, shapes within shapes to any number of levels. When you start the hatch routine, you pick a point within the area you want hatched. The routine then starts from the outer boundary of that area and works its way inwards. If it meets an internal boundary – i.e. a shape inside the shape – it can react in one of three ways:

- The **normal** option stops hatching at the first internal boundary, so that the first inner shape is unhatched. If it meets a further shape within this, it starts hatching again.

- The **outer** option stops hatching at the first internal boundary and leaves everything within this unhatched.

- The **ignore** option hatches everything inside the outer limits of the shape, ignoring internal boundaries.

Figure 5.1 The 'island' options which apply where shapes have other shapes within them. Left to right: normal, outer and ignore.

The patterns available include ANSI and ISO standard hatches and a number of predefined ones. You can also define your own, though that is not something I have room to cover here. The patterns will normally be in the current colour (gradient fills are different), but the colour can be changed later if required.

The scales of the patterns vary, with some being much larger than others. This is not visible from the samples in the dialog box, but is immediately obvious if you try to use them at their default scale. The scale can be set in the dialog box.

To hatch a shape:

1 Click the **Hatch** button on the Draw toolbar.

2 At the **Hatch and Gradient** dialog box, first select the **Type**. Initially there will be only Predefined – User defined and Custom ones can be added later.

3 Pick a **Pattern** by name from the drop-down list using the **Swatch** as a guide, or...

4 Click the [...] button to the right of the Pattern list to open the **Hatch Pattern Palette**. Switch to the **ANSI, ISO** or **Other Predefined** tab, and select a pattern. Click **OK** to return to the **Hatch and Gradient** dialog box.

5 If you want to put the pattern at an **Angle**, set the value.

6 Set the **Scale** now, or wait until after you have previewed it.

Figure 5.2
Picking a pattern – and the samples are no guide to scale. You'll have to wait for the preview to see how they work.

7 Click **Pick Points** 📋 to start selecting the area to be hatched.

8 Click once anywhere inside the area.

9 Right-click to open the shortcut menu.

10 If there are islands within the area to be hatched, select the **Island detection method**.

Figure 5.3 The pop-up menu during the Pick Points stage.

11 Select the **Enter** option to return to the dialog box.

12 Click the **Preview** button to see how your settings work.

13 Click or press [**Escape**] to return to the dialog box to change the hatch or adjust the scale.

Or

14 Right-click to end the routine and accept the hatch.

The hatch object

The hatch does not actually fill the object, in the sense of becoming part of it. It is, in fact, a solid element with the same shape as the original, but quite separate from it. The hatch can be deleted, moved or manipulated independently of its object.

If you click on the hatched area it will be selected – its solid lines become dotted and a handle will appear at the centre.

- To delete the hatch, press [**Delete**] – the original object will not be affected.

- To move the hatch, drag the handle.

- To rotate, mirror or otherwise modify the hatch, use the Modify tools as you would with any other object.

- To change the hatch colour, use the Color drop-down list in the Properties toolbar, as for lines (page 72).

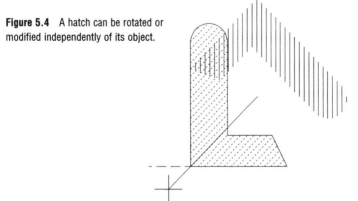

Figure 5.4 A hatch can be rotated or modified independently of its object.

The hatch may be a separate object from its shape, but it remains intimately connected. If you change the boundary of the shape, the hatch will – normally – adjust to fit the revised shape.

Hatches and layers

When a shape is hatched, selecting the hatch is simple enough, but selecting the shape itself is much trickier as the hatch overlies it. The simplest solution is to put the hatch on a different layer. You can then move down to the shape's layer and select it there if you need to modify it. Being on a different layer does not affect the connection with the shape – if its boundary is altered, the hatch's boundary will adjust to match.

Editing the hatch

The hatch pattern and its settings can also be changed. To do that, we need to get back into the Boundary Hatch dialog box.

To edit the hatch pattern:

1 Select the hatch.

2 Right-click and select **Hatch Edit...** from the pop-up menu.

Figure 5.5 Editing an existing hatch – note that the more commonly-used modifying commands can be started from the pop-up menu.

Figure 5.6 The Hatch Edit dialog box is exactly the same as the Hatch and Gradient dialog box.

3 The **Hatch Edit** dialog box will open.

4 Adjust the pattern, scale, size or island detection style, then click **OK**, or preview the hatch and exit from there.

Gradient fills

These are applied in much the same way as hatching. The only real difference is in the way that the fill is defined.

Gradients can use one or two colours. With one colour, the fill varies from the chosen colour through to a lighter or darker version of it. With two colours, the fill varies from one to the other.

The shading can be linear or radial, with variations of each mode, and it can be set at any angle.

To fill a shape with gradient shading:

1 Click the **Gradient** button on the Draw toolbar. The **Hatch and Gradient** dialog box will open at the **Gradient** tab.

Figure 5.7 The Gradient tab of the Hatch and Gradient dialog box.

2 Select **One color,** then pick the colour and use the **Shade > Tint** slider to set the other end of the gradient,

Or

3 Select **Two color** and pick the colours to use.

4 Select the style of gradient – and notice that you can fine-tune the effect by setting the **Angle,** and by turning the **Centered** option on or off.

Figure 5.8 Colours are set in the same way as for lines (see page 72).

Figure 5.9 Select the style, then set the angle to adjust the effect.

5 Click **Pick Points** ⬛.

6 Click once inside the area to be hatched, then right-click. At the pop-up menu, select **Enter**.

7 Back at the dialog box, click the **Preview** button.

8 Click or press [**Escape**] to return to the dialog box to change the hatch or adjust the scale.

Or

9 Right-click to end the routine and accept the hatch.

Exercises

1 Draw a rectangle of 300 by 200, with a smaller rectangle within it. Inside this, draw four circles.

2 Using the Hatch routine, fill each of the circles with solid green or blue, then define a 45° Line hatch and apply it to the outer area and the circles. Your drawing should look like this.

3 Delete the line hatch, then reapply it so that it only fills the outer area.

4 Using the Hatch Edit routine, apply a different hatch or gradient to all the circles.

Summary

*   Closed shapes can be filled with a hatch pattern or with solid or gradient colour.

*   If shapes have shapes within them, the inner shapes can be hatched, or left clear, or alternate between hatched and clear.

*   If a hatched object is deleted, moved or modified, its hatch is deleted, moved or modified along with it. But the hatch can be deleted, moved or modified without affecting the object which it fills.

*   Hatches can be redefined using the Hatch Edit routine.

*   In a gradient fill, the colour shades smoothly from one to another, or a single colour becomes darker or lighter.

06 text

In this chapter you will learn:

- about single line and multiline text
- about bullets and numbering
- how to create tables

Text on drawings

AutoCAD has two types of text – single and multiline. The two have much in common, but with some significant differences.

Both types of text can be used for titles, credits or annotations, and the text can be written anywhere on a drawing, and at any angle. The default size for all text is 2.5 units – and if you have changed the drawing limits significantly, this may not be suitable. Any existing text can be edited, deleted, recoloured, moved or rotated at any point. But...

• Single line text can only be written in the default font and cannot be formatted (apart from its colour). You cannot change the size of existing text – so check the size with the first item of text, to make sure that it is in scale with the drawing. Though you can write several lines of text at one time, so that they sit in a block, they do remain separate lines – you cannot easily rearrange the layout of text, to shorten or lengthen the lines.

• Multiline text can be formatted flexibly – you can apply a different font, colour, size or style to any selection of characters within a text block. The block itself can be reshaped, and the text will flow to fit the new shape.

Single line text

Single line text may have its limitations, but it can be very useful for crisp, clear annotations.

To write single line text:

1 In the Command Line, enter '*text*' to start the command.

Or

• Open the **Draw** menu, point to **Text** and select **Single Line Text**.

2 Pick or enter the coordinates for the start of the text.

3 You will be prompted for the height. If the current setting is suitable, press [**Enter**], otherwise enter the new value.

4 You will be prompted for the angle of rotation. Use the mouse to indicate the angle, or enter a new value, or press [**Enter**] to accept the last-used angle.

5 The I-beam cursor will appear on the drawing. Type the text, pressing [**Enter**] at the end of the line.

6 Type more lines, if required, pressing [**Enter**] after each.

7 Press [**Escape**] to end the routine.

To edit single line text:

1 Click on the text to select it, then right-click on it.

2 Select **Text Edit...** from the pop-up menu.

3 The text will be given a coloured background to indicate edit mode. Click into it to locate the cursor and edit as required.

Side elevation   Side elevation

4 Press [**Escape**] to end.

To modify a single line text object:

1 Select the text.

2 Click on the appropriate tool on the Modify toolbar.

3 Move or rotate the text object as you would any object.

Figure 6.1 Three examples of single line text – one line was being moved when this screenshot was taken.

> ## Wrong size text?
>
> If your single line text is the wrong size, hard luck – you cannot change it! You will have to delete it, and rerun the Text command – setting a new size value at the start. If it is a long line, use [Ctrl]+[X] to delete the text, then [Ctrl]+[V] to paste it into the Command line when you repeat the job.

Multiline text

To write new text:

1 Click on the **Multiline Text** tool **A**.

2 Draw an outline where the text will go.

3 A text window will open and the Text Formatting toolbar will appear. Type the text as normal.

4 To format the text, select the words then use the drop-down lists and tools on the Text Formatting toolbar.

5 If the text area is too narrow, drag on the arrows at the end of the ruler to widen it.

6 Click the **OK** button or click anywhere on the workspace outside the text object to close the text window and the Text Formatting toolbar.

7 To edit the text or change the formatting, select it then right-click and select **Mtext Edit...** to reopen the text window.

As an object, multiline text is more flexible than a single line. When you select the object, you will see that it has a handle at each corner – which means that you can resize it, as well as move or rotate it.

To resize the text object, drag on any handle, pulling it inward or outward as required. Note that this only changes the size of the object – if you want to change the size of the text, you must edit it and use the Text Formatting toolbar.

Bullets and numbering

If you have lists in your multiline texts, you can label them with bullets, numbers or capital letters. As with other formatting, these can be applied before or after you type the text.

To type a labelled list:

1 On the Formatting toolbar, click ⦿ for numbers, or ⦿ for bullets or ⦿ for letters to turn them on.

2 Type your text items, pressing [Enter] after each. The label will be in place at the start of the new line.

3 Click ⦿ or ⦿ or ⦿ to turn the formatting off.

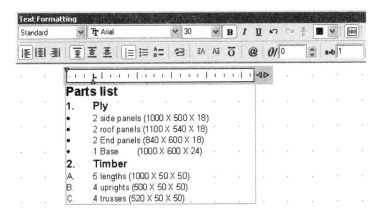

Figure 6.2 Lists. Here there is an outer, numbered list with two subordinate lists – one with bullets, the other with letters. The outer list has been set in bold and a larger type size to emphasize the structure.

To change the formatting of a list:

1 Take the text object into edit mode, if it is not already there.

2 Select the items to be changed.

3 Click 🔢 or 🔢 or 🔢 to turn the format on or off.

Lists within lists

If you have sublists within an outer list, the numbers/letters in each sublist will restart from 1 or A, while the outer list will run in a single sequence.

Tables

In earlier versions of AutoCAD, if you had wanted to set out a table of information, you would have had to draw a grid, using the Line and Rectangle tools, then add single or multiline text objects. Now there is an easier way – you can have tables. Compared to the table facilities in Word, AutoCAD's are fairly crude but at least it's quicker than doing the job by hand.

Text formatting is not handled very well. The simplest way to format your table is to define the text styles for the whole table – its Title, Header and Data rows – before you start to construct it. Alignment and number formats for selected rows, columns or blocks of cells can be changed easily enough later, but text formats can only be changed one cell at a time.

You should also note that the [Tab] key is the most reliable way to move around a table when you are entering or editing text.

◆ [Tab] takes the cursor into the next cell to the right, or – if you are at the end of a row – to the first cell in the next row.

◆ [Shift] + [Tab] takes the cursor back to the left, or up a row.

◆ [Enter] moves the cursor to the cell below.

If you click the mouse to move into the next cell, this will throw you out of editing mode.

To create a table:

1 Click the 🔳 **Table** tool on the Draw toolbar to open the **Insert Table** dialog box.

Figure 6.3 The Insert Table dialog box. Column width and row height can be set now, but it's simple enough to change these after the data is in place.

2 Select a **Table Style name** from the drop-down list. At first there will be only one – *Standard*.

3 Make sure that **Insertion Behavior** is set to *Specify insertion point*.

4 Set the number of **Columns** and **Rows**. (You can add or delete to change the table size later if need be.)

5 Click **OK**.

6 Click on the workspace to locate the top left corner of the table. The table will appear with row and column headers, and the Text Formatting toolbar floating close by.

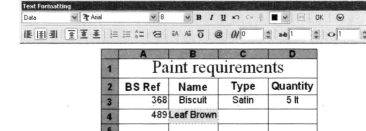

Figure 6.4 Creating and formatting the table data.

7 Type in the title text. Press [**Tab**] to move to the next cell.

8 Fill in the headers and data, using [**Tab**] to move around.

9 If you want to change the default text formatting in any cell, select the text then set the type, size, colour or whatever as required.

Formatting table layout

Text formatting can only be performed one cell at a time, and only from within the editing mode; other types of formatting can be applied more easily. You can set the alignment, border style and data type format for the whole table, or for a row or column or any size block of cells.

To set the alignment:

1 Select the cells to be formatted.

2 Right-click and point to the Cell Alignment entry.

3 Click on an alignment style.

> **Tip!**
>
> To select the whole table, click on any grid line.
>
> To deselect the table, press [Escape] twice.

To format the borders:

1 Select the cells.

2 Right-click and point to the **Cell Borders...** entry.

Figure 6.5 Defining borders.

3 Set the **Lineweight** and **Color**.

4 Click an **Apply to** button: ⊞ All lines; ⊡ Outside only; ⊞ Inside only; ⊞ No borders.

5 Click OK.

If you want to apply one style to the outside borders and another to the inside lines, then run through the process twice.

To set the data type format:

1 Select the cells to be formatted.

2 Right-click and point to **Format…**

3 Select the **Data type**.

4 Select the **Format** and any other options, as applicable – they vary.

5 Click OK.

Figure 6.6 Options vary – only the General and Whole Number formats do not have any options.

Table styles

If you don't like the Standard table style, you can redefine it or define your own styles.

Every table style has three elements, Title, Header and Data, each of which has its own set of properties, including text style, alignment, data type format and borders.

To define a table style:

1 Open the **Format** menu and select **Table Style...**

2 Click [New...] to open the **Create New Table Style** dialog box.

3 Type a name for the new style and click [Continue] to open the **New Table Style** dialog box.

4 Select the Text Style from the drop-down list. If there are no suitable ones – and at first there are only three basic styles – click [ ] to define a new text style.

5 At the **Text Style** dialog box, click [New...] and type a name for your style.

Figure 6.7 Defining a new table style – the contents are identical on the three tabs.

Figure 6.8 Creating a new text style. Only the font type, style and size, and a few special effects are defined here. Colour, alignment and other aspects of the formatting are set in the Table Style dialog box.

6 Set the font name, style and height – and any **Effects** if wanted – then click [Apply] then [Close].

7 Back at the **Create New Table Style** dialog box, set the **Text color, Fill color** (background of cell), **Alignment** and **Border** options.

8 Click the **Column Heads** tab, and repeat from step 4, then again for the Title tab.

9 Click **OK** to close and save the style.

If you later want to edit the style, go back to the **Table Style** dialog box, select it and click [Modify...]. This will open the **Modify Table Style** dialog box which is exactly the same as the **Create New** one.

Exercises

1 Take any existing drawing and add a title to it with single line text of a suitable size.

2 Take any existing drawing and create a simple title block, with the headings 'Title', 'Client', 'Drawn by' and 'Date'. These should be formatted in Arial. Enter 'XXX' for the text under each heading, formatting it in Courier.

3 Use a table to create the same title block. Was that easier?

4 Explore the table-based commands on the shortcut menu. Insert and delete rows and columns to adjust the shape of your table. Play with Merge Cells – select a block of two or more cells before accessing the menu.

Summary

- ◆ AutoCAD has two types of text – single and multiline.

- ◆ Single line text can't be formatted but is handy for notes.

- ◆ Multiline text can be formatted, edited, moved or resized easily.

- ◆ Lists can be formatted with bullets, numbers or letters.

- ◆ The table routines offer a quick way to layout tables of information.

07

dimensions

In this chapter you will learn:

- how to add dimensions to lines, angles and arcs
- how to use leaders
- how to modify dimensions
- about dynamic dimensions

Adding dimensions

AutoCAD has a set of tools that can calculate and display the dimensions of the lines, curves and angles of your drawing. There is a different tool for each type, but all produce the dimension text and arrowed lines to show what it refers to. The size and style of the dimension text, arrows and lines can be adjusted as necessary through the Dimension Style dialog box.

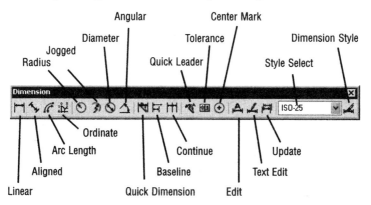

Figure 7.1 The Dimension toolbar.

Linear dimension

On horizontal and vertical lines this will give you the length. It can also be used on angled lines, but will then give the X (width) or Y (height) distance between the points at the ends of the line.

1 Click on the **Linear Dimension** tool ![icon].

2 Click on one end of the line to be measured, then on the other – a new line will appear.

3 Pull the dimension line out and click when it is in clear space.

Aligned dimension

This gives the length of any straight line, drawing a dimension line parallel to the one being measured. Its obvious use is with angled lines, but it works equally well on horizontal or vertical ones.

1 Click on the **Aligned Dimension** tool .

Figure 7.2 Adding a linear dimension.

2 Click on one end of the line to be measured, then on the other – a new line will appear.

3 Pull the dimension line outwards from the drawing and click when it is in clear space.

Figure 7.3 Adding an aligned dimension.

Radius and diameter dimensions

These can be used on any arc or circle, and work in the same way except for two differences. The Radius dimension line starts in the centre of the arc and the text has 'R' at the start; the diameter line runs its full width and the text is prefixed by 'Ø'.

The line can be extended beyond the arc if you want the text to be written outside.

1 Click on the **Radius** 🔾 or **Diameter** 🔾 **Dimension** tool.

2 Click anywhere on the arc and drag around it to set the angle of the dimension line.

3 Draw out from the arc to set the length of the line and the position of the text.

Figure 7.4 Radius and diameter dimensions.

Jogged

This gives the radius, but writes it on a jogged line, so is worth knowing about for when annotation space is at a premium. The dimension line is in a distorted 'Z', starting at any point on the arc and going to any point within it. The positions of the text and of the jog can be set to suit the layout. Compared to a Radius, a Jogged dimension is fiddly to set up.

1 Click on 🔾 the **Jogged Dimension** tool then click anywhere on the arc to fix that end of the dimension line.

2 Click anywhere within the arc to fix the other end of the line. The offset of this point from the normal radius line will be the distance between the jogged lines.

3 Move along the line until the text is in a suitable place, then click to set it down.

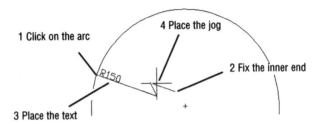

1 Click on the arc

4 Place the jog

2 Fix the inner end

R150

3 Place the text

+

Figure 7.5 You need to fix four points to create a Jogged dimension.

4 Drag the jog line along and click when it's in the right place.

Arc length

This gives you the length of an arc, or of part of an arc.

1 Click on the **Arc Length** tool .

2 Click anywhere on the arc to be dimensioned.

For the whole arc:

3 Drag the dimension out into position and click.

Or for part of an arc:

4 Type 'p' and press [En-

Figure 7.6 Arc length dimension – here, it is the whole arc.

471,24

+

ter].

5 Click at the point where the dimension is to start.

6 Click at the point where it is to end.

7 Drag the dimension out into position and click.

Angular dimension

Figure 7.7 Adding a dimension for a partial arc.

145,8

+

This shows the angle between two lines. These do not necessarily have to meet at a vertex.

1 Click on the **Angular Dimension** tool 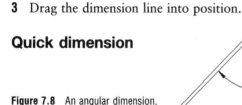.

2 Click on the first line, then on the second – a curved dimension line will appear.

3 Drag the dimension line into position.

Quick dimension

Figure 7.8 An angular dimension.

This tool allows you to set a series of linear dimensions at once, along the same dimension line.

1 Click on the **Quick Dimension** tool 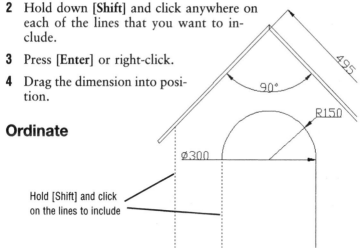.

2 Hold down [**Shift**] and click anywhere on each of the lines that you want to include.

3 Press [**Enter**] or right-click.

4 Drag the dimension into position.

Ordinate

Hold [Shift] and click on the lines to include

Figure 7.9 Quick dimension – setting lines.

Deleting dimensions

If a dimension is no longer needed, it can be deleted – simply click anywhere on its lines or text and press [Delete]. Those created by quick dimension can be deleted individually.

Figure 7.10 Quick dimension gives you the lengths of lines or the differences between the ends of successive lines.

dimension

The Ordinate Dimension tool gives you the X or Y coordinate of a point. This can be useful in itself, but it can also serve as a basis for baseline dimensions (our next topic).

1 Click on the **Ordinate Dimension** tool 📐.

2 Click on the point that you want to label.

3 Drag the line out as required.

Figure 7.11 An ordinate dimension – this drawing originates at Y = 0.

Baseline dimension

This produces additional dimensions from a given start, and has two distinct modes of operation.

- If you start from an ordinate dimension, it produces a series of ordinate dimensions in the same plane.

- If you start from a linear dimension, it produces extensions along the same line.

A little experimentation will help to make things clearer.

Starting from an ordinate dimension:

1 Use the **Ordinate Dimension** tool to display the X or Y co-ordinate of the point you want to use as the base.

2 Click the **Baseline Dimension** tool ⊟.

3 The ordinate dimension should have been selected automatically – if it is not selected, click on it now.

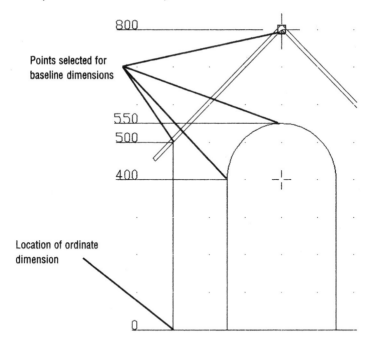

Figure 7.12 Dimensions based on an ordinate dimension – note that the texts are automatically aligned with the base dimension.

4 Click on the points for which you want to add a dimension.

5 Press [Escape] to exit from the baseline dimension routine.

Starting from a linear dimension:

1 Use the **Linear Dimension** tool to show the length of the line.

2 Click the **Baseline Dimension** tool .

3 Click on the end of the line which you want to use as the base.

4 Click on the points for which you want to add a dimension – the new text and lines may overlap the original dimension.

5 Press [Escape] to exit from the baseline dimension routine.

6 If a dimension overlaps another, click on its text to select it – the text and line will become dashed.

7 Draw the dimension text out or along into clear space, then click elsewhere to deselect it.

Figure 7.13 When starting from a linear dimension, new baseline dimensions are placed as extensions of the same line – which means that their texts often overlap.

Leaders

A leader is a multiline caption with an arrowed line pointing to a feature on the drawing.

1 Click on the **Quick Leader** tool .

2 Click on the object that you want to label.

3 Drag and click to create a line from the drawing.

4 If a second line is required – perhaps to angle around another object – drag and click to create it.

5 Right-click to end the line-drawing part of the routine.

6 The Command Line will prompt for the text width. Type a value or right-click to accept the default.

7 You will be prompted for the text. Type the caption into the Command Line, or right-click to get the editing and formatting display as for multiline text (page 93).

♦ If necessary, the caption and lines can be moved, adjusted or deleted later in the same way as any other objects.

Roofing felt

Figure 7.14 A leader with a formatted caption.

Tolerance

This places a feature control frame, to show acceptable deviations of form, position or other aspects of a feature.

The frame can be shown with or without a leader line.

To add a tolerance frame with a leader line:

1 Click on the **Quick Leader** tool .

2 The Command Line will prompt for the first leader point or [Settings]. Type 'S' to open the **Leader Settings** dialog box.

3 Select **Tolerance** as the **Annotation Type** and close the box.

4 Click on the object that you want to label and draw the leader.

5 Carry on as for a frame without a leader (see below).

To add a tolerance frame without a leader line:

1 Click on the **Tolerance** tool – the **Geometric Tolerance** dialog box will open.

2 Click on the **Sym** field to open the **Symbol** dialog box.

3 Select a symbol to show the type of tolerance.

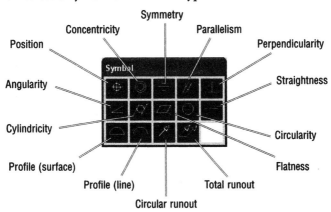

4 Enter the value for **Tolerance 1**.

5 If this applies to the diameter, click the black square on the left to show the diameter symbol (Ø).

6 If a material condition applies, click on the square to the right and select a symbol.

7 Repeat steps **4** to **6** for **Tolerance 2** if required.

8 Add one or more Datum references and complete the dialog box as required.

9 Move the new feature control frame into position.

10 If you decide that a leader line is needed, add a leader as normal, but right-click or press [**Enter**] instead of typing in text.

Figure 7.15 A feature control frame showing the position tolerance. This leader line was added afterwards.

Default settings

When you change the settings on things like the leader annotation type, the new setting becomes the default. Keep this in mind next time you use the tool.

Dimension style

You can control the style, size, colour and position of – and even whether or not to display – the dimension lines, arrows and text.

1 Open the **Dimension** menu and select **Dimension Style...** to open the **Dimension Style Manager** dialog box.

Figure 7.16 The dimension and extension lines are all optional. Text can be horizontal or aligned with its dimension.

2 Highlight a style (if only ISO-25 is visible and you want a choice, select **All Styles** in the **List** box) and click **Modify**.

3 The **Modify Dimension Style** dialog box will open. Work through the tabs, setting the options. Click **OK** at the end.

• **Lines** controls the length and colour of dimension and extension lines. You can suppress the display of any of the lines.

- **Symbols and Arrows** sets the style of arrowheads and the placing and size of centre marks and the arc length symbol.

- **Text** controls the style (the font and formatting), size, colour, position and alignment of text.

- **Fit** options specify what to do when there is not enough room for the text and arrows on dimension lines. Either can be omitted or the text can be moved beside or over the line.

- **Primary Units** set the format and accuracy of the values for the normal linear and angular dimensions.

- **Alternate Units** can be displayed if required, e.g. feet and inches on a metric drawing. You can turn the display on/off and set the format and the relationship to the primary units.

- **Tolerances** can also be displayed, with the same or different upper and lower values.

New styles

When you modify the current dimension style, the changes will be applied to all existing and any future dimensions. This may not be what you want. If you want to use different dimension styles in a drawing, you can create a new style. If this is set as the current style (in the Dimension Style Manager dialog box), existing dimensions will be unchanged. You can return to the dialog box and switch to a different style whenever it is needed.

If a style is to be used for certain types of dimensions, that can be written into its definition.

To create a style:

1 At the **Dimension Style Manager** dialog box, click **New**.

2 Give the style a name, and select which dimensions it is to be used for (if relevant).

3 Click **Continue**.

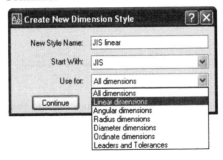

4 The **New Dimension Style** dialog box is exactly the same as the **Modify** box. Work through the tabs then click **OK**.

Exercises

1 Take any existing drawing and use the dimension tools to measure and label all the main dimensions.

2 Change the style of the new dimensions. Format the text in Times New Roman, colour the dimension and extension lines blue, and use open blank arrowheads.

3 Take any existing drawing and add leaders to identify the materials or parts of the drawing.

Summary

* The dimension tools will calculate and display the dimensions of any lines, angles or arcs, or the X or Y coordinate of a selected point.

* Leader lines and arrows can be used for labelling drawings.

* Tolerance values can be displayed.

* You can control the size, style, colour and position of dimension lines, arrows and text.

08

layers

In this chapter you will learn:

- how to create layers
- about the properties of layers
- about layer filters
- how to change an object's layer

What are layers?

Layers are the AutoCAD equivalent of overlay sheets in paper-based drawing offices. In a building drawing, for example, you might have one layer for the brickwork and woodwork, one for the wiring, one for the plumbing, and so on. As layers can be hidden, you can display or print any single layer or combination of layers, to give an uncluttered view of selected features. You can assign a colour, linetype and lineweight to a layer, which helps to identify sets of features and gives consistency to their appearance.

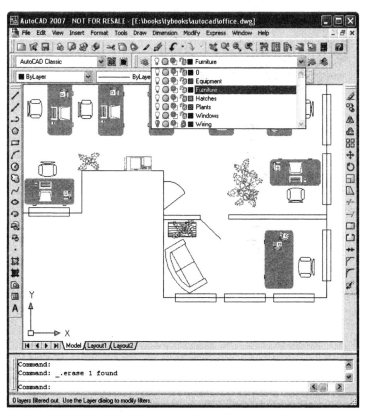

Figure 8.1 In this office drawing, the walls, windows, wiring, furniture, equipment, hatches and plants are all on separate layers. The drop-down list on the Layers toolbar can be used for changing between layers and setting their properties.

The Layers toolbar

The main part of the Layers toolbar is a drop-down list where you can see and control the key properties of layers.

- **Freezing** makes layers invisible, but also has a deeper impact. When a layer is frozen, AutoCAD completely ignores it when regenerating and redrawing a model. **Thaw** the layer to bring it back into active use. A layer can be frozen in the current viewport only, or in all viewports. (See page 154 to find out about viewports.)

- **On/off** simply toggles the visibility of a layer. When turned off, a layer is not displayed or plotted. Freeze layers that are not likely to be needed for a while; use On/off to hide layers on a temporary basis.

- **Lock** prevents objects on a layer from being edited or deleted.

- **Colour** shows the default colour for lines and hatches on the layer. You cannot change the colour from here.

To change properties using the toolbar:

1 Click on any of the property icons, the layer name or the drop-down arrow on the right to open the list.

2 Click on the layer name to switch to a different layer.

3 Click on the icon to toggle between on/off, freeze/thaw or lock/unlock. You cannot freeze a layer while it is current – if necessary switch to another layer first.

Figure 8.2 The Layers toolbar. To make an object's layer current, first select the object, then click the toolbar button.

Figure 8.3 Two views of the same drawing. In the top one, the furniture, equipment, hatches and plants layers have been turned off so that the structural features can be seen more clearly. In the bottom view, some structural features have been hidden so that the layout of furniture and equipment is more obvious.

Creating layers

When you start a new drawing, it has only one layer, 'Layer 0'. New layers can be created at any stage. As objects can be moved from one layer to another, you can create a layer before drawing the objects on it, or afterwards.

Layer 0 has the default settings for colour (white – or black if the background is white), linetype and lineweight. When a layer is created, it will have the same settings as whichever existing layer is selected at the time, or the default settings if no layer is selected.

Layers are created in the **Layer Properties Manager** dialog box. This has a small set of tools for managing layers, and displays the full range of layer properties. These include Linetype, Lineweight, Plot style and Plot (on/off) which are not shown on the Layers toolbar – you may need to scroll the display across to see the properties on the far right of the set.

To create a new layer:

1 Open the **Format** menu and select **Layer...**

Or

• Click the **Layer Properties Manager** tool on the **Layers** toolbar.

Figure 8.4 The Layer Properties Manager dialog box. The width of the columns can be adjusted by dragging on the dividing lines in the header row.

2 If you want the layer to start with the same settings as an existing one, select it now, otherwise click in the blank area of the window so that no layer is selected.

3 Click **New**.

4 A new layer will be listed. Replace the default name '*Layer1*' (or whatever number) with a more meaningful name. Set the layer's properties.

5 With the toggles – **On, Freeze, Lock** and **Plot** – click on the icon or the checkbox in the Details area to switch them on or off.

6 To set the **Colour, Linetype** or **Lineweight,** click on the icon to open the related dialog box, or open the drop-down lists in the **Details** area to select an option there.

7 To change the name, double-click on the name in the main list, or click into the **Name** field in the Details area. Edit as with any other text.

8 Click **OK** to close the **Layer Properties Manager** dialog box when you have finished.

To delete a layer:

1 If there are any objects on the layer, delete them, or move them to other layers (see below).

2 Open the **Layer Properties Manager** dialog box.

3 Select the layer.

4 Click X the **Delete** button.

Layer filters

If you have a lot of layers, it can be useful to restrict the display in the Layer Properties Manager. Property filters allow you to do this. When one is applied, only those layers that meet certain criteria are displayed. The criteria can be set on any properties – whether a toggle is on or off; the choice of colour, lineweight or style; whether the name contains specified characters or digits.

To create a property filter:

1 In the **Layer Properties Manager** dialog box, click the **New Property Filter** tool.

2 In the **Layer Filter Properties** dialog box, start by typing a name to identify the filter.

3 To set a criterion, first click into the row beneath a property heading.

4 With **On, Freeze, Lock** or **Plot**, a list will drop down showing the on and off symbols – select one.

5 With **Colour, Linetype** or **Lineweight**, a dialog box will open – select the required property from there.

6 To filter on the **Name**, type the characters to match, starting and ending with '*'. For example, '*work*' would select 'brick**work**', 'block**work**', 'wood**work**', '**work**shop'.

7 If you want to set alternative criteria, e.g. two colours, then click into the row below and specify the other property there.

8 Click **OK** when you have done.

9 Back at the **Layer Properties Manager** dialog box, select the filter from the list in the left-hand pane.

Objects and layers

New objects are always created in the current layer, whatever that may be. An organized person will set the layer, then create the objects for it. Not all of us are that organized, and when we are focused on what we are drawing, we may lose sight of where we are drawing it. It is also all too easy to be mistaken about what layer is current – if an object is selected, its layer is displayed on the Layers toolbar.

To move objects between layers:

1 Select the object.

2 Drop down the **Layers** list.

3 Click on the layer that you want to move the object onto.

Sometimes, this doesn't work and the object will stay resolutely on the same layer despite you best efforts! There is a solution.

To move objects between layers using the Properties:

1 Select the object.

2 Right-click and select **Properties** from the pop-up menu.

3 Open the **Layer** drop-down list and select the new layer from there.

4 Close the **Properties** palette if it is no longer wanted.

Exercises

1 Create a simple drawing or open an existing one and add extra details, text, dimensions and hatches, placing these on different layers.

2 Give each layer a different colour, and change the linestyle and weight on the dimensions layer to make its lines more distinctive.

3 Look back at other existing drawings and see if the use of layers would make them more manageable.

Summary

- Layers are like overlay sheets in drawings on paper. They can be turned on or off, or locked to prevent changes.

- You can see and control the key properties of layers from the Layers toolbar.

- New layers are created in the Layer Properties Manager dialog box.

- Property filters can be used to select which layers are to be included in the Properties Manager display.

- You can move an object from one layer to another.

09 blocks

In this chapter you will learn:

- how a set of objects can be made into a block
- how to insert blocks into drawings
- about the DesignCenter and DC online

Blocks

A block is a set of objects that can be handled as a single unit, and which is identifed by name. If you have several instances of the same component in a drawing, you could draw it once, convert that to a block, then insert copies of the block as required.

The larger and more complex the drawing, the more useful you will find blocks. It is much simpler to insert a named block than to select a set of objects, especially if those objects are close to or overlap others which are not part of the set.

Making blocks

First double-check the objects that are to be converted into a block. Make sure that everything is in place and that if any formatting (see Chapter 4) is required, it has been done. You can edit blocks, but it is far simpler to get it right in the first place.

To make a block:

1 Select the objects.

2 Click the **Make Block** tool 🖫 on the Draw toolbar.

3 At the **Block Definition** dialog box, enter a **Name** to identify the block.

4 Click the **Pick point** button 🖳 then pick a point within or near the objects to act as a base point. This will be used for locating the block when it is inserted or moved.

Or

♦ Type the coordinates of the base point.

5 If you need to add to or change the set of objects, click 🖳 to select them.

6 Type a **Description** if it might be useful in the future.

7 Leave the other settings at their defaults and click **OK**.

Inserting blocks

If you can see the block in your working area, you can copy it with the usual techniques. If it is not visible, you can locate it by name using the Insert Block routine.

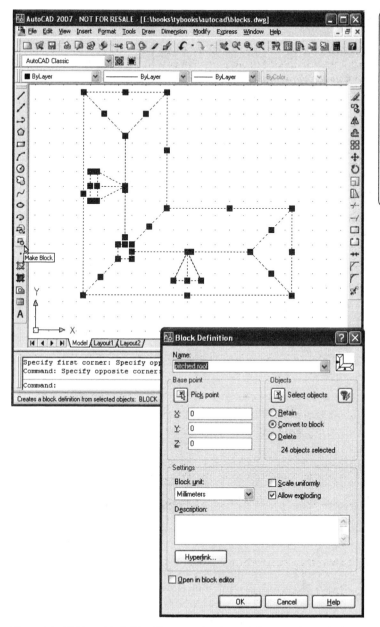

Figure 9.1 Making a block. The objects can then be copied or moved as a single unit.

You can set the position, scale and rotation by typing the values into the dialog box or by manipulating the block on screen.

1 Click the **Insert Block** tool on the Draw toolbar.

2 Select the block from the **Name** drop-down list.

3 For the **Insertion point**, tick the **Specify On-screen** checkbox or enter the X, Y (and Z if in 3D) coordinates.

4 To set the **Scale** factor, tick the **Specify On-screen** checkbox or enter the X, Y (and Z) values.

5 To set a **Rotation**, tick the **Specify On-screen** checkbox or enter the angle.

6 If you want to be able to edit the components of the block after placing it, tick the **Explode** checkbox.

7 Click **OK**.

Figure 9.2   Insert a block. Only the Insertion point is essential.

Inserting drawings

A complete drawing can be inserted into another. Use the Insert Block tool to start, then Browse for the drawing file at the Insert dialog box, and insert it as if it were a block.

Editing blocks

A standard block is a single unit. If you have placed a block in a drawing and want to change any of its component lines or shapes you must first explode it to return it to a set of normal drawing elements, which can be modified as normal. The original block definition is not affected by this.

If you have several instances of a block in a drawing and want to make the same change to all of them – and to any future ones – you can edit the block definition. This can be done in the workspace or the Block Editor. Let's start with in-place editing.

1   Select the block, then right-click on it and select **Edit Block In-place** from the shortcut menu.

Figure 9.3 Note the fourth set of commands – you can scale or rotate a block, but only as a complete unit.

Or

•   Open the **Tools** menu, point to **Xref and Block In-place Editing,** select **Edit Reference In-place,** then click on the block. (In AutoCAD jargon, a block is an external reference.)

Figure 9.4 If the block contains other blocks, set the 'select nested objects' option; otherwise, just click OK.

2 At the **Reference Edit** dialog box click **OK**.

The **Refedit** toolbar will appear.

Add to working set

Remove from working set

Save reference edits

Close reference

3 To edit a component line or shape, select it and move or modify using the normal tools.

4 To remove a component from the block, select it and click **Remove from working set** ⬜.

5 To add a new component to the block, select it and click **Add to working set** ⬜.

6 When you have finished, click **Save reference edits** ⬜ or **Close reference** ⬜ to revert to the design before editing.

• Simply closing the **Refedit** toolbar does not end the editing routine. You must save or discard the changes to end.

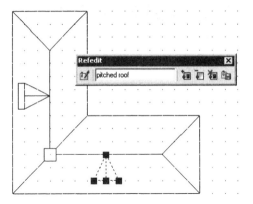

Figure 9.5 Editing a block. The selected component can now be moved, modified or removed without affecting the other components.

The Block Editor

If you are just editing a single standard block, the Block Editor offers no real advantages – it is essentially the normal workspace but with a different coloured background and a couple of extra sets of tools. The Editor comes into its own in two circumstances. If you want to edit a number of blocks, this offers a simple way of reaching them; and if you want to create or edit dynamic blocks – of which more shortly – this has the tools.

1 Open the **Tools** menu and select **Block Editor**.

2 At the **Edit Block Definition** dialog box, select the block to edit then click **OK**.

Figure 9.6 This can be called up from within the Block Editor to select blocks for editing.

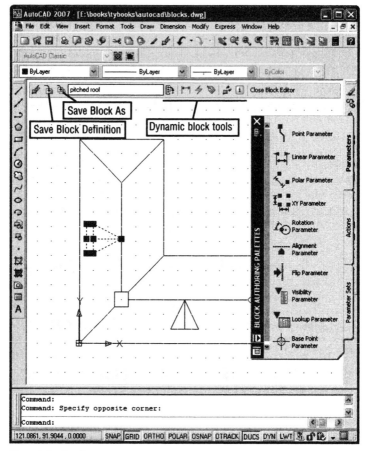

Figure 9.7 The Block Editor – look for the new toolbar at the top of the workspace.

3 In the Block Editor, edit the drawing in the usual way.

4 When you have finished, click **Save Block Definition** to write the changes into the original block.

Or

5 Click **Save Block As** to save the edited drawing as a new block, leaving the original unchanged.

6 Click **Close Block Editor** to return to the workspace.

Dynamic blocks

A dynamic block is one where you can change the length, angle or other aspect of one or more of its components, after it has been placed into a drawing. The changes made to that copy of the block will not affect any other copies in the same drawing.

There are two stages to adding a dynamic feature to a block: first define the parameter – more or less the same as a dimension – which can be changed, then define the action which can be applied to it. For example, here's how to create a variable width component within a block. This uses the Stretch action, which needs you to specify the parameter to be changed, the grip to associate it with, and the points to be made stretchable. Other actions have different specifications.

1 Take the block into the Block Editor.

2 On the **Parameters** tab of the **Block Authoring Palettes,** click on **Linear Parameter**.

3 Pick or enter the coordinates of the start point – in this case, the top left corner of the doorway.

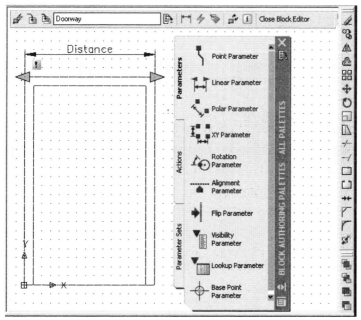

Figure 9.8 Making a block dynamic! First add the parameter to be changed.

4 Set the coordinates of the end point – the top right corner.

5 The label will be lying along the top line – draw it far enough away to be clearly visible. Click it into place.

6 On the **Actions** tab of the **Block Authoring Palettes,** select the **Stretch Action.**

7 Select the parameter to be made variable – the label and lines should be highlighted.

8 Select the parameter arrow to be the grip for the action.

9 Define the rectangle to enclose the points to be affected.

10 Click on each of the objects to be stretched or moved. Right-click when you have selected them all.

11 Click to locate the label – this is only visible in the Block Editor.

12 Save the changes and close the Block Editor.

Figure 9.9 Setting up the action.

When you are back in the workspace, drag on the dynamic grip to change the parameter. In this example, the right-hand side of the block would move, changing its width.

Explore the other actions – some are easier than others to get to grips with. Scale is a good one to start with.

The DesignCenter

The DesignCenter gives you easy access to the blocks and other features of the drawing files on your system – including the very many objects in the sample files that are supplied with AutoCAD. It can also be used to access the huge range of predefined blocks at DC online (AutoDesk's website).

To display the DesignCenter:

◆ On the **Tools** menu, point to **Palettes** and select **DesignCenter**.

The Palette has four panes – three of which are optional:

> **Tree view** shows the folders, which can be opened to show the drawings, which in turn can be opened to show their blocks and other elements.

Toggles: Tree view Preview Description

Hide Tree view Description Preview

Figure 9.10 The DesignCenter – use the toggle switches to control the display.

Preview gives you a close-up of the selected block.

Description gives the specification or a brief description of the selected block.

The main pane shows the contents of the selected folder or drawing. As in My Computer in Windows, the contents can be viewed as small or large icons, a list or 'details' (which actually has no details at all!). Large icons are probably the most useful.

Inserting a block

Inserting a block is straightforward – at the simplest you can just drag it from the DesignCenter onto the drawing. The tricky bit is getting the scale right, as the drawing that the block is coming from and the one that it is going into may have quite different scales. For example, if you drop in a block from the *House Designer* sample drawing into one started with the default settings, it will be so big that you may have to zoom out to be able to see it!

The solutions are not difficult – you just have to remember that you may need to use them.

To insert a block with drag and drop:

1   In the DesignCenter, open the folders to reach the drawing, then open the drawing to get the list of elements, and finally select the *Blocks* heading to display the blocks.

2   Select the block and drag it onto the drawing.

3   Release the mouse to drop it onto the drawing.

4   If the DesignCenter is in the way – click the **Hide** button.

5   Click on the block to select it. You should see a single blue handle on or near it. Drag on this handle to move the block.

Figure 9.11   Blocks from other drawings may need to be scaled to fit your drawing.

6 If the block is the wrong size, use the **Scale** tool (page 57). You may find it simpler to type a scale factor, rather than use the mouse, especially if you want to make the block smaller.

Scale and units

If you are going to bring a number of blocks in from other drawings, and they are all or most at the same scale, you can set the default scale factor in the Drawing Units dialog box. If you will be using samples from the DesignCenter in a standard metric drawing, you should find that they fit better if you set the scale to *Centimeters* instead of the default *Millimeters*.

To set the default scale:

1 Open the **Format** menu and select **Units...**

2 In the **Insertion scale** area, drop down the **Units to scale** list and select an appropriate unit.

3 Click **OK**.

4 Insert a block to test the effect, and try a different unit if it comes in at the wrong scale.

DC Online

AutoDesk runs a DesignCenter Online service, offering a wide selection of 2D and 3D blocks, produced by its own people and by outside suppliers. Individual blocks can be downloaded free of charge, or you can buy them in sets at very reasonable rates.

To insert blocks from DC Online:

1 In the DesignCenter, switch to the **DC Online** tab.

Figure 9.12 A lot of drawings of standard components are available at DC Online.

2 If you are not already online, you will need to connect to the Internet at this point.

3 Wait for the Category Listing to download. It will appear as a folder display in the left-hand frame and as a simpler listing in the top pane.

4 Open the folders to reach those that contain blocks – these are normally at the third level down.

5 Click on an icon in the contents display to see its preview and details in the lower pane.

6 To capture the block, click the **Save this symbol as...** link and save it as a drawing file on your system.

• The saved block can be inserted through the DesignCenter, using the Tree view display to locate the drawing's folder.

Exercises

1 We are going to make a spiral staircase.

Draw a circle with a radius of 10 units, centred at 100,100.

Draw a polyline using these coordinates: 100,100; 30,100; 39,145; 100,100. Use the Trim tool to remove the ends of the polyline within the circle.

Copy the polyline using a polar array, centring it at 100,100 and making 10 copies over an angle of –270°.

Make the drawing into a block, naming it 'spiral'.

2 Insert the spiral block into another drawing, adjusting its scale to suit, and rotating it as necessary.

3 Explore DC Online, downloading at least two blocks and inserting them into your drawings.

Summary

* A set of lines and shapes can be made into a block, for easier handling and copying.

* When inserting a block into a drawing, you can set its position, scale and angle.

* A block can be exploded into its component parts.

* With a dynamic block, one or more of its dimensions or other properties can be changed after it has been inserted into a drawing.

* The DesignCenter gives you easy access to the blocks on your system and at DC Online.

10

from sketch to plot

In this chapter you will learn:

- about plans and elevations
- about plotters, paper sizes and scaled output
- how to set up layouts
- about viewports
- how to preview and plot

Sketches

All drawings start in the head. The question is how best to get them from there into AutoCAD. One of the best methods is through sketches. They need not be accurate – that's what AutoCAD is there for – but they will enable you to get an idea into a workable shape.

The first stage is to translate the idea (Figure 10.1) into a rough sketch (Figure 10.2). This should should show the overall shape and dimensions.

Figure 10.1 The idea.

Figure 10.2 The first sketch.

Orthographic projection

Though AutoCAD can display models in 3D, the majority of technnical drawings are still 2D, and normally use *orthographic projection*. This shows the object from the top (the plan), the end or side (side elevation) and the front (front elevation).

Figure 10.3 Orthographic projection – how the plan, front and side drawings relate to the object.

If we apply the orthographic principles to our 3D sketch, we can derive these sketches:

+ **The plan** – a top-down view of the object, showing the widths and lengths of its components (Figure 10.4).

+ **The front elevation** – how the object looks when seen flat-on from the front. This should be marked with the widths and heights of its parts (Figure 10.5).

- **The side elevation** – how the object looks from the side (left or right). Lengths and heights should be on here (Figure 10.6).

Figure 10.4 The plan.

Figure 10.5 The front elevation.

Figure 10.6 The side elevation.

- You may also need one or more **sections** through the object if there are features inside that cannot be seen from the front or side.

The sketches do not have to be complete. In the example here, the width of the sloping roof is not known. It could be calculated, but there is no point in spending time doing this as AutoCAD can work out dimensions for you.

Model space and paper output

So far, we have only been working on screen, so we have only had to think about the size of the model space. In the working world, plans are normally printed out onto paper and drawn to certain standard scales, such as 1:10 or 1:200. This means that we have to think about paper sizes and drawing scale when setting up the model space.

The first question is 'What size is model space?' What are the outside dimensions of the object, or if your drawing is of the plan, front and side elevations, what is the total length and width of the space that they would be laid out in? Once again, a paper sketch helps – all you need is a rough sketch with the main dimensions.

Figure 10.7 A sketch of the layout, with the outside dimensions.

In the example in Figure 10.7, the model space must be at least 600 + 1100 long, and 800 + 700 wide. Allowing an extra 200 each way for dimension text, the model space needs to be at least 1900 by 1700.

I'm using millimetres, but AutoCAD can work in any units. The commonly used drawing units are *Architectural* (feet and inches with fractions), *Engineering* (feet and inches with decimal fractions) and *Decimal*, which is normally used with metric units but you can have any unit at all – feet, cubits or whatever. The type of unit, and how they are displayed does not really become important until you start to add dimensions. At the setup stage it is enough to work out the size of your model space in whole units.

Paper sizes

There are three sets of paper sizes in common use: ISO, ANSI and Architectural. The sets are very similar, with the largest size around three foot by four foot, and four smaller sizes, each half the size of the one before. (Architectural has an extra large size.)

	ISO		ANSI		Architectural
					Large E	36 × 48"
A0	841 × 1189mm	E	34 × 44"	E	30 × 42"
A1	594 × 841mm	D	22 × 34"	D	24 × 36"
A2	420 × 594mm	C	17 × 22"	C	18 × 24"
A3	297 × 420mm	B	11 × 17"	B	12 × 18"
A4	210 × 297mm	A	8½ × 11"	A	9 × 12"

What size of paper will the drawing be printed on?

Printers and plotters rarely work right up to the edge of the sheet. What is the actual size available for your drawing? If you don't know, you can find out when you first start to plot a drawing, as AutoCAD will tell you the plottable area of the sheet.

Standard scales

You can use any scale you like for your drawing – AutoCAD will happily work with any scale value – but the working world tends to use certain scales. These are nice round numbers if you are working in metres, less so for feet and inches.

Typical use	Scale	Scale factor
Area plans	1 = 200mm	200
Building plans	1 = 100mm	100
House plans	1 = 50mm	50
Details	1 = 20mm	20
Fine details	1 = 10mm	10
Area plans	$1/16'' = 1'$	192
Building plans	$1/8'' = 1'$	96
House plans	$1/4'' = 1'$	48
Details	$1/2'' = 1'$	24
Fine details	$1'' = 1'$	12

Calculating the scale

Time to get the calculator out! You need to divide the length and breadth of the minimum model space by those of your paper. It doesn't have to be a very accurate result, because you are then going to take the highest of the two values and round this up to the nearest standard scale.

For example, my dog kennel drawing needs a minimum model space of 1900 by 1700, I am plotting on A4 paper and the plotter leaves a margin of 7mm all round. The plottable size is therefore 283 × 196.

Length scale = 1900 / 283 = 6.7

Width scale = 1700 / 196 = 8.7

Largest scale = 8.7

Next standard scale = 10

If you now multiply the usable paper size by the scale, you will get the maximum available model space – in this case, 2830 × 1960. If you set your drawing limits to this, you will have a clear correlation between the model space and the paper size.

Let's look at an example in imperial measures. We are drawing house plans with an overall size of 45 × 38', the paper is Architectural D (24 × 36") but with a ½" margin all round.

As the plans are in feet and the paper size is in inches, we must convert the plan lengths to inches.

Length scale = (45 × 12) / 35 = 15.4

Width scale = (38 × 12) / 23 = 19.8

Largest scale = 19.8

Next standard scale = 24 = ½" = 1'

Multiplying the paper size by the scale (and dividing by 12 to give the results in feet), we find that we can draw plans up to 70 × 46' on Architectural D paper at ½" = 1'.

Know your limits

If you regularly use the same size of paper, it will be worth spending a few minutes working out the maximum drawing limits at the standard scales for that paper.

Setting up and drawing

Once you have worked out the size of your model space, you can set up a file for the drawing.

1 Use **File > New** and select the **Start from scratch** option. Set the Default settings to Metric or Imperial as required.

2 Set the drawing units and drawing limits to suit your plan and the model space – see pages 10 to 13 if you have forgotten how.

3 Turn on the grid, and the snap, if required, and start drawing!

♦ While you are simply drawing in model space, you don't have to think about scale or the paper output – just keep within your drawing limits.

4 When you start to add dimensions and/or text, scale matters again. Adjust the size of the text and arrows to suit your scale (see Chapter 7).

You can print directly from model space, but if you want properly scaled and professionally presented output, you should use layouts.

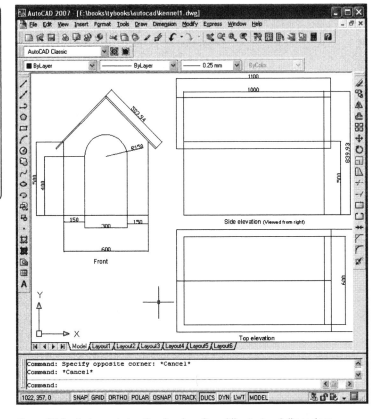

Figure 10.8 A plan and elevation drawing after adding text and dimensions.

Layouts

A layout is a view of model space, perhaps with annotations or other enhancements, prepared for output to a plotter or printer. It can show the whole of the drawing or just a part of it. It can include text, dimensions and additional drawn items that are not present in model space. For instance, you would normally place the title block on a layout, rather than in model space where it would just be clutter.

Each layout is designed for a specific plotter/printer and paper size, and displays the drawing in a specific view. It is possible to change the plotter, paper and view later, but any changes may affect the way that the material fits onto the layout. Unless there is a good reason for changing, it is probably better to set up a new layout with the required settings.

To create a layout from scratch:

1 Click on a layout tab. The **Page Setup Manager** may appear (it can be turned off). If it does, check that the right layout is selected and click **Modify**.

2 At the **Page Setup** dialog box, first select the **Printer/plotter**.

3 Select the **Paper size**.

4 Set the **Drawing orientation** as required.

5 Set the **Plot scale** to the design scale of the drawing. Depending upon the size of the drawing and of the paper, the **Fit to paper** option may be available.

6 Click the **Preview...** button to see how it will look. If necessary, go back and adjust the settings.

7 Click **OK** to close the dialog box.

The model space will be outlined. Depending upon the paper and layout settings, there may be significant space around this. If you add title blocks or annotations in the margins, they will only be present on that layout.

Figure 10.9 Print preview of a simple layout. This has had a title block table added.

Accessing model space

It is possible to go into model space through a layout – double-click on the drawing area to go in, and outside the drawing area to return to the layout level. Use this to adjust the view of the drawing – once you are in model space you can zoom and pan over the drawing to bring a part into focus. You can also draw or add notes while you are there, but if you are not careful you will add items to model space that are only wanted on the layout. If you want to add to the drawing, go to the Model tab and do it there.

Viewports

A viewport divides the screen into two or more areas so that you can look at your model in different ways at the same time. Viewports can be created in model space and in layouts – the technique is the same in both.

The screen can be divided into up to four viewports. Any or all of the resulting viewports can then be further divided likewise. You also have a set of predefined viewports to choose from, and can create your own.

To divide the screen:

1 Open the **View** menu, point to **Viewports** and select the number of viewports.

2 You may be asked to choose **Horizontal** or **Vertical** division.

3 If required, click into a viewport to be subdivided and repeat the steps.

Or

4 Open the **View** menu, point to **Viewports** and select **New Viewports...**

Figure 10.10 This screen has been divided vertically into two viewports. The left side has been selected and is about to be divided again.

5 The **Viewports** dialog box will open with the **New Viewports** tab at the front.

6 Click on the name of a viewport to see a preview of the screen division.

7 When you find a suitable layout, click **OK**.

To save a viewport for later use:

1 Go to the **New Viewports** tab.

2 Select 'Active Model Configuration' if it isn't already selected.

3 Enter a name and click **OK**.

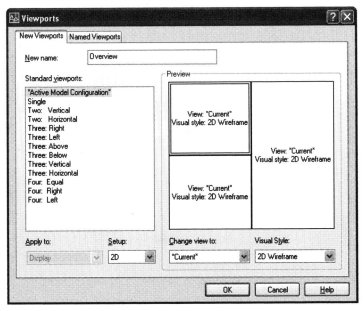

Figure 10.11 The Viewports dialog box when saving a viewport.

Plotters and plotting

The plotters and printers installed in Windows are available in AutoCAD, but for best results (see the boxed item below), you should install them in AutoCAD through the Plotter Manager.

1 In the **Tools** menu, point to **Wizards** and select **Add Plotter...**

2 Work through the wizard, responding to the prompts.

3 At the Plotter Model stage, select from the lists of **Manufacturers** and **Models**, or click **Have Disk...** to use the installation disk supplied with the device.

Figure 10.12   If your device is not on the list and you do not have a disk for it, you can still use it if it is installed at Windows level.

4 Carry on through the wizard – you will probably find it useful to run the calibration routine at the end.

Problems of scale

In theory, if you have set up your model space and pages properly, the drawing that you have set to 1 = 10, or whatever scale, should be plotted (or printed) to that scale. However, if you are using a Windows plotter/printer driver, rather than an AutoCAD one, the output may not be exactly to scale.

Preview and plot

When you have finished adding to the layout, you can plot it directly, or check the preview first – this is worth doing, even though the layout gives a very good idea of the plotted output.

1 Right-click on the layout's tab and select **Plot...** to open the **Plot** dialog box.

2 Check the settings, then click **Preview...** to see the layout as it will look when plotted.

3 Click **Apply to layout** to save the plot settings with the layout so that you do not have to reset them next time you plot.

4 Click **OK** to send the layout to the plotter.

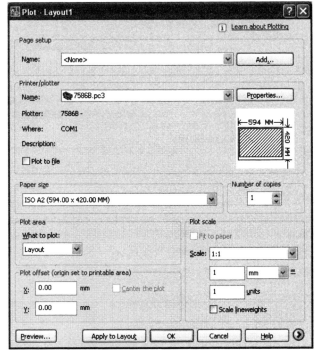

Figure 10.13 The Plot dialog box.

The Layout Wizard

The wizard offers a quick way to set up a layout, and provides the simplest way to get a ready-made title block into a drawing.

1 In the **Tools** menu, point to **Wizards** and then select **Create Layout...**

2 The first few steps cover the **Printer**, **Paper Size** and **Orientation** – make your selections as usual.

3 At the **Title Block** step, if you want to use one, select a ready-made block suitable for your paper size and orientation.

4 At the **Define Viewports** step, select **Single** to use the current view – the other options are for advanced work.

5 At the **Pick Location** step, click **Select Location** to go into the layout and draw a rectangle where you want the drawing.

Figure 10.14 Defining the location for the drawing area.

6 Click **Finish**.

7 To edit the title block, double-click on it. The **Enhanced Attribute Editor** dialog box will open.

8 Work through the tags, clicking on each in turn and typing your details in as the Value. Click **OK** when you have done.

9 If you want to move the drawing area on the layout, click and drag on its border to move the area.

10 If you want to resize the drawing area, click on its border then drag on a handle to make the area larger or smaller.

Figure 10.15 A layout produced by the wizard.

Publishing

If you want to output more than one sheet, the Publish routine is more efficient than Plot. This lets you select several sheets – which should have their plot options set already – and plot them in one operation. It also offers the option of publishing the drawings as a DWF file, which can viewed by the DWF Viewer. This free software from AutoDesk is designed to allow your clients to view and mark up your drawings, making the review cycle faster and cheaper.

Exercises

1 Take an existing drawing, go to its layout tab and send it to your plotter using the default settings. Examine the result.

2 Find out what you can about the plotters and printers which you can use. What paper sizes can they handle? What are their printing areas?

3 Use the Layout Wizard to set up a drawing for a selected plotter. Include a template and edit the attributes in the title block.

4 Explore the Publish command, especially the DWF option.

Summary

- It often helps to start by sketching your ideas on paper.

- The majority of technnical drawings are 2D, and use orthographic projection.

- If you want to plot to a standard scale, you have to think about paper sizes and drawing scale when setting up the model space.

- There are three sets of paper sizes in common use: ISO, ANSI and Architectural.

- A layout is a view of model space, prepared for output to a plotter.

- A viewport divides the screen into two or more areas.

- Plotters and printers should be installed in AutoCAD, using the Plotter Manager.

- You can preview a layout before sending it to the plotter.

- The Layout Wizard offers a quick way to set up a layout, especially if you want to add a title block.

drawing in 3D

In this chapter you will learn:

- about 3D drawing modes
- the Z coordinate and the X, Y, Z axes
- how to draw wireframes in 3D
- about 3D views and 3D orbit
- how to plot 3D drawings

3D modes

AutoCAD has three different 3D drawing modes, and you cannot easily switch objects from one mode to another. In practice, you need to decide which mode is appropriate for the job and use that. The modes are:

* **Wireframe** is an extension of standard 2D drawing into the third dimension. Objects are defined and displayed in terms of edges and points, but have no surfaces. Wireframe drawing is very time-consuming, but at least it uses the same tools and techniques as 2D work. We will use the rest of this chapter to look at wireframes.

* **Surface** drawing defines objects in terms of their faces using a polygonal mesh. As each unit of the mesh is flat, rounded surfaces are not truly curved. Surface models are about as time-consuming as wireframes to construct, and are created with the special Surface tools and techniques. There simply is not enough space in this book to cover these.

* **Solid** models are built up from a set of basic 3D shapes – box, wedge, cylinder, sphere, cone and torus. These can be adapted and combined to construct any other shape. Of the three modes, solids are the simplest to use, though you have to switch from AutoCAD Classic to the 3D Modelling workspace. We will look at some of these shapes in Chapter 12.

The Z coordinate

In AutoCAD, the X, Y, Z coordinate system is screen-based – not absolute. The X coordinate always refers to the position left–right across the screen, the Y coordinate is the vertical position and the Z coordinate is the position in or out of the screen.

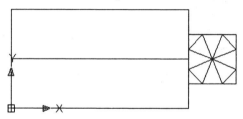

Figure 11.1 Looking down on the plan of a building

So, if you are looking at an object from the top, X is its width, Y its length and Z its height above the ground.

But if you look at it from the front, X is the length, but Y is the height and Z its width (or depth into the screen).

Figure 11.2 Looking at the same building from the front – X and Y are still in the same directions on the screen, but now refer to different dimensions on the object.

This could be confusing, as the same point will be at 20,40,60 or 20,60,40 or 60,40,20 depending upon which way you are looking at it. However, it does make drawing simpler as long as you are working in the same plane, because you only need to specify the X and Y coordinates.

An example will help to get your head round the key concepts. We are going to draw two squares – one above the other – by entering their coordinates. Notice that you give all X, Y and Z values for the first point, but only X and Y for the second. AutoCAD assumes that it is in the same plane.

1 Start a new drawing.

2 Click the rectangle tool. Enter the first corner as 0,0,0 and the second as 100,100.

Figure 11.3 In isometric views, the bottom axes (X and Y in this example) are set at an angle of 30°, and parallel lines stay parallel – these are not perspective views.

3 Click the rectangle tool again. This time, enter the first corner as 0,0,50 and the second as 100,100.

4 Open the **View** menu, point to **3D Views** and select **SW Isometric**.

5 Try each of the 3D Views to see how the object looks.

Figure 11.4 A wireframe drawing in an isometric view. The 3D View options also include flat-on views from the top, bottom, left, right, front and back. Notice how the direction of the X, Y, Z pointers is determined by the previous 'flat-on' view.

3D Polyline

The circle, arc, line and other drawing routines all behave in much the same way as the rectangle. You fix the first point in 3D space, then give only 2D coordinates for the later points. The object is then drawn flat-on to the screen at the depth set by the first Z coordinate.

The Draw menu includes a **3D Polyline** tool, which can be used to draw straight-sided objects in 3D space. The standard Line tool can also be used to draw in 3D space, but it results in a series of linked lines while the 3D polyline is a single element.

Try this – it will draw an (almost) regular octahedron.

1   Start a new drawing, or erase the objects from the last trial.

2   Open the **Draw** menu and select **3D Polyline**.

3   Type these sets of coordinates into the Command line:

50,50,-75	0,0,0	100,0,0
100,100,0	0,100,0	0,0,0
50,50,75	100,100,0	50,50,-75
100,0,0	50,50,75	0,100,0

4   Now view it through the 3D Views.

◆   As this is a regular shape, the isometric views all look the same, as do those from the sides or from the top and bottom. Never mind, there are other ways to view 3D objects.

5   Open the **View** menu, point to **Orbit** and select **Free Orbit**.

6   A green circle, with little circular handles at each quadrant, and a coloured X, Y, Z axes icon will appear. Drag on any part of the screen and the object will rotate in 3D space.

Other orbits

The Orbit submenu also offers Constrained and Continuous options. In both of these, you drag on a vertex or any other point on the object, which can give a better correlation between the mouse movement and the movement of the object. In Continuous, the object keeps rotating when you release the mouse button. Click again to stop it moving.

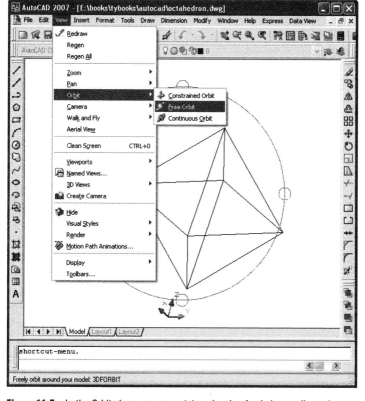

Figure 11.5 In the Orbit views you can rotate a drawing freely in any dimension.

Tips for drawing in 3D

Though you are using almost the same tools, drawing in 3D is different from drawing in 2D and you do need to change your approach.

* Never forget that there is a Z coordinate – and that it will refer to different dimensions depending upon which way you are viewing model space.

* Apart from the Line, the standard drawing tools draw flat in the current plane, but you can set the Z depth when specifying the first coordinate.

* It takes a lot more coordinates to define a 3D shape! And compared with 2D work, the coordinates are more likely to

be repeated. There will typically be three or more lines meet-
ing at each vertex, and you may have to specify that vertex
for each line.

♦ Drawing with the mouse is more difficult, because it is hard
to control the cursor position in 3D space from a 2D mouse
mat. It is not really feasible to pick coordinates – most will
have to be entered through the Command line.

But...

♦ Object Snap works just as well in 3D space. Turn it on, then
once a vertex is in place, you can join other lines to it quickly
using the mouse. You need to be in an isometric view for
this. Look at the spire on the church drawing in Figure 11.4
(page 169). To construct this, I first drew an 8-sided polygon
on the top of the tower (by specifying the centre location and
radius). I then switched to the 3D polyline tool, specified the
position of the top of the spire, then drew the lines between
the vertices of the polygon and the top of the spire using
Object Snap.

♦ If you draw something in the wrong place, you can reposition it with the Move command – but specify the base point
and the displacement point in the Command line, and check
which way round the X, Y, Z pointers are facing before you
do this!

♦ You can also reposition objects by editing their coordinates
in the Properties palette.

Plotting 3D drawings

As a 3D drawing is as flat on the screen and on paper as a 2D
drawing, it's no surprise that the same techniques are used when
plotting. However, note these two points.

When you create a layout, the drawing will appear in the View
mode that was current in model space. If required, you can change
to a different mode now – simply open the View menu and pick
a 3D View option.

There is a simple way of creating a plan-and-elevation plot. At
the Define Viewports step of the Layout Wizard there is an option **Std. 3D Engineering Views**. Choose this to get a top, side,
end and isometric view on a single plot.

Create Layout - Define Viewports

Begin
Printer
Paper Size
Orientation
Title Block
▶ Define Viewports
Pick Location
Finish

Autodesk

To add viewports to the layout, specify the setup type, scale, and (if applicable) the rows, columns, and spacing.

Viewport setup
○ None
○ Single
⦿ Std. 3D Engineering Views
○ Array

Viewport scale:
Scaled to Fit

Rows: 2   Spacing between rows: 0.1
Columns: 2   Spacing between columns: 0.1

< Back   Next >   Cancel

Figure 11.6 The Std. 3D Engineering View is the simplest way to get multiple plots of a 3D drawing.

Figure 11.7 In this layout, dimensions have been added to the standard 3D engineering view. If required, you can change any or all of the views – click into the view to select it, then pick a new mode from the View menu.

Exercises

1 Either draw a wireframe model of a house of your choice, or of the dog kennel. The kennel's dimensions are shown in the screenshot on page 152. You can work out most of the coordinates from that. If the bottom front left corner is at 0,0,0 then the corners of the roof are:

50,450,-50; -300,850,-50; -650,450,-50;

50,450,1050; -300,850,1050; -650,450,1050.

2 Plot your drawing using Engineering view layout.

Summary

- AutoCAD has three different 3D drawing modes: wireframe, surface and solid.

- The X,Y,Z coordinate system is screen-based – not absolute.

- The View menu includes a set of 3D view options.

- Lines, rectangles and circles can be drawn in 3D, but only in the same plane as the screen.

- With 3D polylines you can construct objects anywhere in 3D space.

- The Std. 3D Engineering Views option is the simplest way to get multiple plots of a 3D drawing.

12

3D solids

In this chapter you will learn:

- how to define and use 3D solids
- how to combine solids to create new shapes
- about the lighting options
- how to render an image

3D modelling

AutoCAD has a comprehensive system for drawing solids. It would take a whole book to describe it fully – there is only room here to give an introduction to its possibilities. We will look at how basic shapes can be defined, then combined to create new shapes, and also explore ways of viewing 3D models. If you follow the examples given here, you will finish up with a solid model of the church that you saw as a wireframe in Chapter 11. (I like the irony of modelling a 13th century building in 21st century software.) Let's get started.

1 Start a new drawing from scratch.

2 Select **3D Modeling** from the list on the **Workspaces** toolbar.

Or

3 Open the **Tools** menu, point to **Workspaces** and select **3D Modeling**.

4 The Dashboard and the Tool Palettes will be present, docked on the right of the workspace. You might want to drag these off to make them floating, then turn on **Auto-hide**.

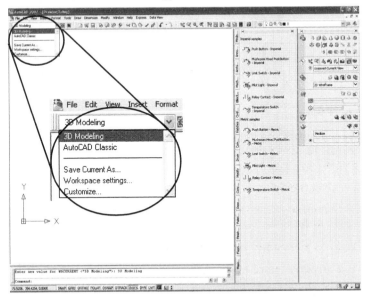

Figure 12.1 The palettes do not leave you much room for drawing!

Solids tools

You will find the tools for drawing solids on the top of the Dashboard. We will only be using the five tools labelled here. Explore the others later when you have an hour or two to spare.

Figure 12.2 The Dashboard has all the tools that you need for normal work in 3D.

Sphere

We will start with the sphere, because it gives a good illustration of the display options for solids. The tool draws a perfect sphere around a point.

1 Click the **Sphere** tool on the **Solids** toolbar.

2 Switch to a suitable view – Front view is good when starting on a model.

3 Enter the coordinates of the central point.

4 Enter the radius of the sphere.

♦ You should see a circle with an inner circle and crossing diameters. In a flat-on view it doesn't look much like a sphere.

5 Select an isometric view from the **Views** list in the Dashboard.

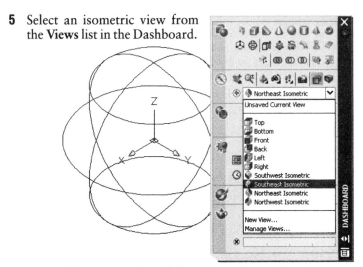

* You will see an outline of the sphere, drawn from five inter-linked circles. This is the standard 3D wireframe display.

We can get a better-looking sphere by changing the **Visual style**. Open the drop-down palette and select **Conceptual** or **Realistic**. These both give the object a surface.

3D Hidden – useless for spheres!

2D Wireframe

Conceptual

Realistic

3D Wireframe

There are no spheres in our model, so you might want to re-move the test sphere – select it and press [Delete].

Box

To define a box, you first give the position of one corner. You can then specify its size in three different ways:

by giving the X, Y, Z position of the opposite corner;

by giving the length (X), width (Y) and height (Z);

by specifying 'cube' and giving the length of a side.

And remember that the direction of the X, Y, Z axes depend upon the view you are in.

To create a box:

1 Click the **Box** tool on the Dashboard.

2 Switch to **Front** view.

3 Enter the position of a corner (usually the bottom left front), e.g. 0,0,0.

4 Specify the opposite corner, e.g. 150,80,100 – this produces a box 150 long by 80 wide and 100 high.

5 Open the **View** menu, point to **3D Views** and select an isometric view.

♦ If you want to make the church, you will need a second box for the tower. This should start at 150,20,0 and should be 40 long, 40 wide and 150 high.

Visual styles manager

You can edit many aspects of the visual styles – colour, style and density of lines in wireframes, use of shadows, surface colours and shading in solids, and much more.

Use Tools > Palettes > Visual Styles to open the Visual Styles Manager and explore the settings.

Cone

A cone is defined by the position of the centre of its base, the radius of the base and the height of the cone. It will be drawn with the base in the same plane as the screen – so make sure that you are in a suitable view when you start.

1 Click the **Cone** tool on the Dashboard.

2 Switch to the appropriate view – Top in our example.

3 Enter the position of the centre of the base – to draw one at the top of our tower you should enter 170,40,150.

4 Enter the radius, e.g. 20.

5 Enter the height, e.g. 50.

6 Switch to an isometric view so that you can see how it looks.

Wedge

Wedges can be awkward! They are drawn with the base in the same plane as the screen and sloping down across the screen (the highest end will be over the start position).

They can be defined in several ways. The simplest is probably to give the opposite corner of the base, and then the height. But however you define a wedge, it is still very easy to create one that slopes the wrong way, or that faces the wrong way. If it slopes the wrong way, delete it and start again. If it faces the wrong way, it can easily be turned round – as you will see if you work through the next example. We are trying to create a roof for the main part of the church model.

Figure 12.3 These wedges all have the same length, width and height but are quite different shapes.

To make a wedge:

1 Pick a view where the base of the wedge will be flat on to the screen – Top in our example.

2 Click the **Wedge** tool on the Dashboard.

3 Enter the coordinates of a corner at the high end of the wedge – 0,40,100 for our example.

4 Enter the coordinates of the opposite corner of the base – e.g. 40,190,100. (This creates a wedge 40 wide by 150 long.)

5 Enter the height – for our roof this should be 50.

6 Switch to the **SW Isometric** view.

♦ You should have a wedge of the right shape for (half) the roof, but in the wrong place. No problem! This can be easily rotated into place.

To rotate a solid:

1 Click on the solid to select it.

2 Make sure that **Object Snap** and **Polar** are turned on.

3 Select the **Rotate** tool from the **Modify** toolbar or menu.

4 Click on the corner of the solid at 0,40,100.

5 Using the rotate guideline, swing the wedge through 270° to bring it into the right place.

♦ Create the other half of the roof by constructing a wedge of the same shape at 150,40,100 and rotating it through 90°.

Figure 12.4 Shapes can be easily moved and rotated. The techniques are the same as for 2D objects, but you need to get into a suitable view first so that you can see what you are doing.

Cylinder

The last solid we will be using in our model is the cylinder, and we need this to create the arches above the doors and windows.

Like the solids, a cylinder is drawn with its base in the same plane as the screen. As the cylinders in this model will come out from the front wall, we need to view our drawing from the front. This example is the first stage in constructing the main door in our church model.

To create a cylinder:

1 Switch to a suitable view, use **Front** in this case.

2 Enter the coordinates of the centre point, e.g. 25,50,-5.

3 Enter the radius, e.g. 15.

4 Enter the height – 10 for this example.

To complete the doorway, we need a box of the same width as the cylinder to fill the space down to the ground. Construct a box 30 wide by 50 high by 10 deep. (Start from 10,0,-5.)

Figure 12.5 We now have a doorway that is stuck half-in and half-out of the front of the church, but what we actually need is the same shape cut out of the front wall. And that brings us nicely to the next topic.

Combining solids

If two or more solids touch or overlap, they can be combined to create a single new shape. There are three tools:

♦ **Union** joins the solids into one, absorbing any overlaps.

♦ **Subtract** removes the overlapping volume, creating a cavity. (The rest of the subtracted solid is also removed completely.)

♦ **Intersect** removes everything except the overlap.

We will use all three in our model. You will find the tools in the top section of the Dashboard.

Union   Subtract   Intersect

Union

This is probably the simplest of the tools. Use it to join the two parts of the doorway.

To join solids:

1 Click the **Union** tool in the Dashboard.

2 Hold down [**Shift**] and click on each of the solids to be joined – they should all be shown in dotted lines. If you select a solid by mistake, click on it again to deselect it.

3 Right-click to create the union.

♦ Join the two roof wedges in the same way.

Figure 12.6   The doorway solid after the union operation.

Subtract

To subtract one solid from another:

1 Check that the solids are intersecting in the right way.

2 Click the **Subtract** tool.

3 Click to select the solid from which you want to subtract the overlap (the main body of the church, in our example). If there are several solids, hold [**Shift**] while you click. Right-click when you have done to move on to the next part of the operation.

4 Select the solid(s) to be subtracted (the doorway), and right-click when you have done.

♦ You should now have a hole the same shape as the overlap.

Figure 12.7 Subtracting the doorway from the main block creates an opening – unfortunately there's nowhere to go as the building is a solid block! We need to do another Subtract to carve out the inside. I'll leave you do that.

Let's take a second example. I want to make the end of the roof slope. If we create a big box overlapping it at an angle, we can use the Subtract tool to cut off the end.

1 Go to **Front** view.

2 Construct a box, starting at 0,100,0 (i.e. the bottom corner of the roof), with the opposite corner at -80,180,-80.

This is bigger than is needed, but it doesn't matter.

3 Rotate the box around its start point, so that it overlaps the roof by 15° or more.

4 Click on the **Subtract** tool.

5 Select the roof as the base from which to subtract.

6 Select the block as the solid to subtract.

Figure 12.8 Rotating the box into position to subtract it from the roof shape.

Intersect

I want a pointed arch on the windows of the church model –
and I know I'm mixing Norman and early Perpendicular architectural styles, but this is only an example! On a 2D drawing,
this could be created with two interlocking arcs. In 3D, we can
produce the shape by intersecting two cylinders. Try this.

1 Go to **Front** view.

2 Construct a cylinder with the centre at 55,50,0, radius 10,
height 10.

♦ It should appear on the church wall to the
right of the doorway.

3 Create a second cylinder with the centre at 65,50,0, radius 10, height 10.

♦ The two should overlap as shown
here – this is seen in SW isometric
view.

4 Click the **Intersect** tool on the Solids Editing
toolbar.

5 Hold down [**Shift**] and select the two cylinders.

6 Right-click to complete the operation.

This doesn't look much like an arched window!

1 Add a box to complete the shape. It should be
10 wide, 20 high and 10 deep, starting at
55,30,0 (working in **Front** view).

2 Join the two shapes together with the **Union**
tool.

3 The 'window' is on the surface of the wall. It
needs to be pushed back into it. No problem!

4 Select the window shape.

5 Click the **Move** tool on the Modify toolbar.

6 Enter 55,30,0 as the base point.

7 Enter 55,30,-5 as the second point.

♦ Yes, we could have sunk the cylinders and the box into the
wall when we created them, but then you wouldn't have got
to try out the **Move** command!

Copying solids

There are no special tricks here – it is almost identical to copying in 2D. You will find it helps to work in the view which brings the solids into the same plane as the screen so that coordinates are easier to work with. You may also find it helps to have Object Snap turned on. You will need to give the coordinates of a base point, and if you snap to a corner they will be displayed in the Status bar.

Copy the window shape three times along the front of the church, leaving a gap of 15 between each pair. If you use its bottom left corner as the base point, the copy points should be 80,10,-5 then 105,10,-5 and 130,10,-5.

You can now subtract the window shapes from the main block.

You should have a model which looks something like this.

Figure 12.9 The model as in wireframe and conceptual styles. I have added a window and door to the tower – you may like to do the same.

Which visual style?

The more realistic the appearance, the more computing power and time it takes to redraw the screen display, though you may not notice the difference on a small, simple model. As a general rule, stay in 2D or 3D Wireframe mode while building the model, switch into Hidden if you need a clearer overview, and only use Conceptual or Realistic styles when you are preparing the final output. And for this, you might want to add materials, lighting and rendering. Read on!

Materials

These give textures and colours to surfaces. If you installed the optional Materials Library, you have some 300 materials effects, including plastic, glass, stone and wood. (You can use your own images instead of or as well as these.) How you apply a material depends upon whether or not it is already in use in the drawing.

To use a material for the first time:

1 On the **Tool Palettes**, select a palette of materials – if you cannot see what you want on the tabs, click the bottom of the tabs display for a full list.

2 Look through the materials to find a suitable one.

3 Click the image to select the material.

4 Back on the workspace, click on the object(s) that are to have this surface.

5 Right-click or press [Enter] to end.

Figure 12.10 There are more materials on the palettes than just surface effects – have a good browse. And watch the scroll bar – some palettes have far more things than others.

The surface 'materials' are only images, and they may not be quite what you want – for a start, they may be quite the wrong scale for your drawing. This is not a problem. Once the material is in the workspace, it can be edited. The changes will be applied to any material already in use, and be in place for future use.

To edit a material:

1 Click ⊞ the **Materials** button on the Dashboard or use **Tools > Palettes > Materials** to open the **Materials** palette.

2 Select a material.

3 You can change the way it reacts to light by adjusting the Shininess, Refraction Index and Translucency settings. These have more effect on some materials than others.

4 Make sure **Diffuse map** is turned on. These settings control how the image is applied to the surface. Use the slider to adjust the intensity of the image.

5 Click ⊞ to open the **Adjust Bitmap** dialog box.

6 Set the **Units** so that the image is in the same scale as the model, then use the **Width** and **Height** to fine-tune the size – check the material in your workspace to see how it looks.

Once a material is in the workspace, you would normally access it from the Materials palette. Select it again from the Tool Palettes if you want to revert to the original settings, or if you want a second copy of it, to adjust in a different way.

To use a material that is already in the workspace:

1 Select the material in the **Materials** palette.

2 Click ⊞ the **Apply Material to Objects** button.

3 Click on the object(s) that are to have this surface.

4 Right-click or press **[Enter]** to end.

To remove unwanted materials:

1 Select the material in the **Materials** palette.

2 Right-click and select **Purge from Drawing**.

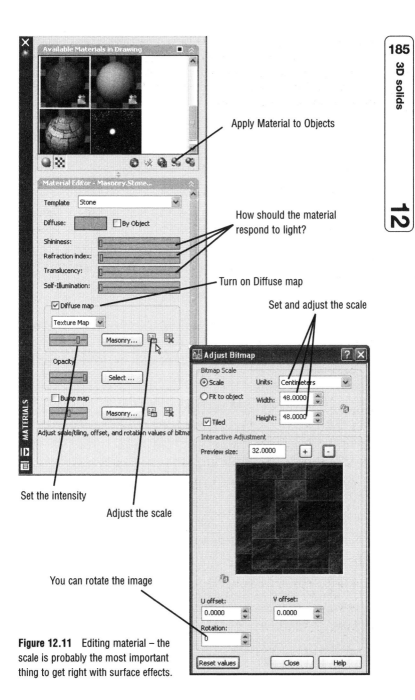

Apply Material to Objects

How should the material respond to light?

Turn on Diffuse map

Set and adjust the scale

Set the intensity

Adjust the scale

You can rotate the image

Figure 12.11 Editing material – the scale is probably the most important thing to get right with surface effects.

Lighting

Lights help to set the scene. The light control panel is the third section of the Dashboard, and initially displays only the minimal set of controls.

* **Lighting mode** switches between default, general, lighting and user-defined 'sun' and lights settings.

* **Sun status** turns the sun on and off – weird concept! And the Date and Time sliders control its position.

* **Lights list** opens the Lights palette.

When you open the panel fully, there are tools for creating lights, changing the geographic location and – my favourite – **Edit the sun.** You can also control the overall colour and brightness here.

Experimentation and close observation are needed to work out how best to light a scene. Start with the sun. Changes made to this are visible straight away.

* Make sure that the lighting mode is set to user light/sunlight before you begin.

To edit the sun:

Either

1 Set the **Date** and **Time** using the sliders.

2 Click 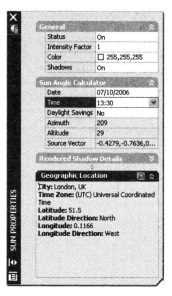 and set the **Geographic Location**.

Or

3 Click 🔳 to **Edit the sun**.

4 Set the intensity, colour, date, time, location and other factors there.

Defining user lights takes a little longer, and the effects are not really apparent until you render the scene – of which more shortly. Here's how to add and set up spotlights. The technique is the same for point and distant lights.

To add spotlights:

1 Click 🔳 **Create a spotlight**.

2 Pick or enter the location for the light.

3 Pick or enter the location of the target.

Picking points in 3D

Using pick to locate a light – or anything else – is just about impossible to do accurately in 3D space. The best approach is to locate it initially in a 2D view, e.g. Top, then switch to an alternative 2D view, e.g. Front, to fix the third coordinate.

4 A menu of options will appear. Click on any to set them – you will be prompted as required. Select **eXit** to end.

5 If the Light glyphs option is on, you will find the spotlights in model space. If you select one, you can adjust its position, target, and the spread of the beam.

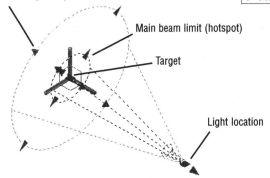

Outer beam (fall off)

Main beam limit (hotspot)

Target

Light location

Figure 12.12 A spotlight glyph with the grips for adjusting locations and beams.

6 Depending upon the surface and the lights, you may or may not need to render before you can see the effect of your lights.

Background

You can give your model a coloured or picture background. The colour can be solid, or a gradient effect, shading across three colours. The picture can be any bitmap image, and can be stretched or tiled to fill the window. We'll use an image. The background is part of a view, not of the model, and is set when defining the view.

To set a background:

1 Select a view for the model and/or use the Pan, Zoom and Orbit tools to set it into position.

2 On the **Dashboard,** open the **Views** list and select **New View.**

3 Enter a name, then turn on **Override default background**.

4 In the **Background** dialog box, set the type to **Image** then click **Browse...** and locate the picture file.

Click to browse for a different image

Override the default

Can be Solid or Gradient colour

Figure 12.13 Setting a background image.

5 Use the **Preview** to get an idea of how the image will look. If it is the wrong size, or you want to recentre it, click **Adjust Image...** and set the scale or offset there.

6 Click **OK** to end.

Rendering

Rendering applies the lighting settings to the model, showing how it interacts with materials and how objects cast shadows on one another. You can see this to some extent with the normal view modes – rendering just does it better, and can take a while to do so.

To render a scene:

1 In the **Render control panel** part of the Dashboard, first set the quality. Select **Draft** for the first look – you may well want to change light settings when you see them in use.

2 Click the **Render** button.

3 The Render window will open, and the rendered image will be built up while you watch.

4 The image is stored as a file, so that you can come back to it later for another look after you have done other renderings.

Figure 12.14 The rendered model on its background. This has been just a quick example to show what is possible – I'm sure that you could do better.

These files are erased when you shut down AutoCAD. If you want keep one for permanent reference, open the **File** menu, select **Save** and store it as normal.

Exercises

1 Start a new drawing and make sure that you are in Top view.

Create a box with the coordinates 0,0,0 and 400,300,200.

Create a cylinder centred at 200,150,0 with a radius of 60 and a height of 200.

Create a second box with the coordinates 150,100,400 and 250,200,600.

Switch to an isometric view then subtract the cylinder from the first box.

Change to a conceptual or realistic visual style.

You should now have a square peg and a round hole!

2 Experiment with these techniques to produce your own 3D models. When you have mastered them, explore the Extrude and Rotate tools – they can turn flat surfaces into 3D solids, allowing you to create more complex objects.

Summary

- AutoCAD has a 3D Modelling mode for drawing solids.

- You can use the tools to create a sphere, box, cylinder, wedge, cone or torus.

- Objects are best created flat-on to the plane of the screen.

- Solids can be modified in the same way as 2D objects, using the tools on the Modify toolbar.

- Where solids overlap, they can be merged in different ways by the Union, Subtract and Intersect tools.

- You can display a model as a wireframe, with hidden lines removed, or with conceptual or realistic surfaces.

- Rendering applies lighting settings to the interaction of objects and to their surfaces.

taking it further

This book should have helped to get you started with AutoCAD, but it won't have made you an expert – there's a lot more to learn before you can claim that label!

The Help system in AutoCAD is very thorough – possibly too thorough. There is so much information that it can take a while to filter the many possible topics to find the one that answers your question. Persevere. The more familiar that you are with AutoCAD, and with its Help system, the easier it becomes to get the Help that you need.

There is lots of help and other resources available online. The Online Resources entry in the Help menu leads to links to the product support, training and customization at Autodesk's web site (www.autodesk.com), and to the Autodesk User Group's site (www.augi.com). You can also get help from and share your ideas with other users through the 30 or so newsgroups devoted to aspects of AutoCAD – look up 'autocad' in the newsgroup subscription routine of your mail and news reader.

If you want recognition of your AutoCAD skills, why not try for a certificate or diploma. In the UK, City & Guilds offers qualifications at several levels, as do other organizations elsewhere. A search for 'AutoCAD' and 'examination' at Google should lead you to your local testing authority.

But the most important thing that you can do to take your AutoCAD expertise further is to experiment and explore. There are so many tools and routines to play with – enjoy them!

index